ONLY Angels CAN Wing It

Liz Curtis Higgs

THOMAS NELSON PUBLISHERS
Nashville • Atlanta • London • Vancouver

To my husband, Bill Higgs,
Ph.D., DAD, and Director of Operations:
Bless you for always being there
to straighten my halo,
dust off my wings,
tune up my harp,
and nudge me off my cloud.
I love you, Sweet Bill!

February 1995

Acknowledgements

My husband Bill once observed that "it takes about ten people to do Lizzie!" Sure enough, none of us do what we do without the help of friends and associates. Never is that more true than when writing a book.

Heartfelt thanks, then, to the eight hundred women who completed surveys, offered stories, and shared their lives with me and, therefore, with all of us. You are a blessing!

Hugs to my friends and heroines in the world of speaking and writing: Florence Littauer, Marita Littauer, Jeanne Robertson, Naomi Rhode, Rosita Perez, Elizabeth Jeffries, Gail Wenos, Luci Swindoll, Patricia Fripp, Maureen Mulvaney, Jolene Brown, Janie Jasin, Cathy Fyock, Connie Podesta, Nancy Coey, Sue Thomas, Patsy Clairmont, Joanne Wallace, Hope Mihalap, Marilyn Heavilin, Linda Pulliam, Pat Vivo, Barbara Johnson, and especially my petite "sister" and precious friend, Glenna Salsbury. Your care-filled craftmanship with the spoken and written word is a joy to behold and a beacon for the rest of us to follow.

A big, beautiful hug to my editors at Thomas Nelson Books: Lonnie Hull DuPont in San Francisco and Sheryl Taylor in Nashville. I appreciate you more than even *words* can say!

Special thanks to my friends at *Today's Christian Woman* magazine, Jane Johnson Struck and Ramona Cramer Tucker, who've also helped me find my "voice" as a writer. Bless you both!

Peace and love to my professional manuscript reader, Lois Luckett, MSW, LCSW, who offered much needed direction, feedback, and encouragement. Your caring touch is on every page.

Grateful bows to my clients and friends in the National Association of Women's Health Professionals who've given me so many opportunities over the years to humor and encourage the women they serve. In particular, I'm indebted to my NAWHP readers: Patricia Thomas, Joyce Kieffer, Evelyn Freeman, and Susan Sanders, who allowed my lengthy manuscript to invade their holidays. Ho ho ho!

Many thanks to Sonya, Pat, Debbie, and especially to Anne Dorton and Pamela Dennison, who, at various times and in numerous ways, held my office together for more than a year while I played at the word processor. You really *are* earth angels!

Finally, a lifetime supply of hugs and kisses to my dear children, Matthew and Lillian, who give me a reason to soar a little higher.

Contents

You Deserve to Know . . .

This book is *not* about how to do more, how to do it better, or how to do it faster; it's not even about how to *do* it, period.

This is a book about putting aside perfectionism so we can embrace grace. To light the way, we'll take a fresh look at an age-old role model from Proverbs. (Good news: she's not perfect, either; she just practices the right things.)

This is also a book full of laughter, stories, and insights offered via surveys completed by eight hundred women from all fifty states. They, too, long for lives that are less stressful, better balanced, and more fun.

This is a book to keep by your nightstand for the end of another had-to-do-it-all day, when the most your weary self can handle is some real-life humor and a gentle tug at your heart. No tips, no lists, no how-tos—you're busy enough already.

This book is what every woman (including me) wants: assurance that we're not alone, we're not crazy, and we're doing the best mortal women can do.

So . . . let's kick off our shoes, find a comfy chair, and start smiling!

1

Measuring Our Wingspan

wing it (an American colloquialism):
to act, speak, etc., with little or no
planning or preparation; improvise
*Webster's New World Dictionary of
American English*

I have been winging it for forty years.

Well, there was that one really organized year when I managed to keep nearly a hundred houseplants alive, walk to work every day, and whip up lots of healthy home-cooked meals because I had no money and steamed vegetables were cheap. That was 1976; it's been downhill since then.

A decade later, I married at thirty-two. The next year brought motherhood and my own business. A second child, a move to the country, and I've been tired ever since. Not only is winging it not working, but my feathers are starting to drop off. Must be hormonal.

Here we are, standing at the threshold of a new millennium, and I'm not sure I've got enough left in me to start another century. The 1950s were too cheerful, the '60s too strange, the '70s too disco, the '80s too driven, and the '90s too politically correct to be any fun. And what are we going to name the next decade . . . the 00s? If we go around calling it *2,001,* I'll keep expecting HAL the computer to show up.

Flying by the Seat of Our Skirts

Depending on when you read this, we may still have time to mend our wings and take some flying lessons from one another before the new century begins. What Sandy from Michigan hopes to find among these pages is "encouragement to keep going when there aren't any other options" and to do so "joyfully, gracefully, and humorously!" Thank goodness she didn't say "perfectly" because, rest assured, angelhood is not my goal; it never has been. We weren't created to be angels. That's their job title alone.

Billy Graham, who should know, says the "concept of angels with wings is drawn from their ability to move instantaneously and with unlimited speed from place to place."[1] I know what you're thinking. That's us, zipping across town in our minivans, clutching directions in one hand and lunch in the other. It makes us amazing, but it doesn't make us angels.

Angels are perfect because God designed them that way. No one has ever worked up to being an angel. They are created beings who can't *not* be angels, but they also can't be human—that's our task. Because they are never lost, they don't need to be found, and they have no need for a shepherd. I'm glad I'm not an angel. I'm very glad I'm a woman.

If angels are messengers—and they are—here's a message from them to us: relax! By design, we are "a little lower than the angels" (Heb. 2:7 NKJV). Perfect is out of the question; practice is just common sense.

What We Need Is an Un-Do List

"People call me an angel because I 'wing it' all the time! Hope your book includes a guilt release!" wrote Jerrie from Tennessee. Guilt is the grease that keeps us sliding toward depression when we should be soaring heavenward. I'm learning to let go of guilt. Conviction? Of course. Contrition? Often. But if "guilt is the gift that keeps on giving," then I intend to leave no forwarding address.

Sara from Colorado made this request: "We can't 'wing it' today—life requires organization. How about some tips on balancing faith, family, and work?" Sounds like a terrific book, but I'm not sure it's this one. Tips, lists, ideas, suggestions, things to check off, tasks to put in motion—most of us already have more of that stuff than we could ever find time to actually do. The August 1994 issue of *Redbook* featured the cover headline, "115 Ways to Be Thin, Rich, Loved . . . and Happy." That's us, looking for joy by the numbers. We tell ourselves, "Just let me get to Tip #115, and I'll be home free!" Oh, sister.

Our purpose here is to stand back from it all for a moment: reevaluate; hold on to what works, and discard what doesn't; consider some proverbial wisdom from the past as we retool for the new century. On second thought, maybe we *will* be talking about balancing faith, family, and work after all. But no tips—just stories. Yours and mine and those of eight hundred kindred spirits. The youngest woman to respond was Stacy from Oregon at age twenty-two; the most mature was Irene from Kentucky, a youthful eighty-seven, who said she had no interest in marriage right now because "I enjoy not having to answer to anyone!"

The Day the Earth Stood Still

Sylvania from Missouri is counting on this book to include "humorous war stories." Can do. I'll affectionately call this one, "The Business Trip from the Bad Place." It was to be my first public presentation of *Only Angels Can Wing It,* in Albany, New York. An audience of nearly six hundred women had assembled, with another six hundred turned away at the door. Numbers don't make me nervous, but a new topic can get me completely unglued.

I planned, I prepared, I practiced. I made sure all the bases were covered on the home front: "Honey, do you have anything going May 24?"

"No," my husband, Bill, assured me, "it's just a regular work day, nothing unusual. I'll be happy to drive the kids to and from school. No problem."

Two weeks before the Big Day, Bill came to me looking sheepish. If he'd worn a hat, it would've been in his hands. "May 24 is primary election day," he informed me. That meant a sixteen-hour grind for him at the television station handling election coverage.

"Time to move to Plan B," I said. "We'll call Mom and Dad."

Bless the in-laws, they could come and stay with the children after school. We were all set.

One week to go, and a note came home in Matthew's backpack: "Be sure to mark your calendars for the evening of Tuesday, May 24, for the Elementary School Music Program!" A small part of me died inside. Not only would I miss our first-grade son's performance, but so would his dad. Well, Mamoo and Papoo and his little sister, Lillian, would be there, so it would be all right. In fact, it would be *special*. Okay, we're fine.

Tuesday morning, May 24: my notes were in order, my clothes were packed, the kids were in school, the baby-sitter was ready for carpool pickup, the grandparents were en route, Matthew's costume was finished, and I was off to the airport, feeling smug. I am Woman, hear me roar.

The flight went smoothly, my kind client deposited me at my hotel room, and at 4:30 I sat down to make the usual touch-base phone call home. That's when it all began to unravel.

The strain in Mamoo's voice on the phone was the first clue. It seemed Lillian had thrown up in the baby-sitter's car on the way home from preschool and was now "hot as an oven." (Understand, my kids are *never* sick except when I travel. Is this a sign?) I sent Mamoo to the kitchen cabinet for the fever-reducing medicine; she returned to the phone to inform me that the bottle was there . . . empty. Directions to the nearest drugstore ensued as I felt my internal hinge about to spring. Promising to call back in an hour, I hung up and tried Bill at work, knowing he was up to his ears in election coverage pandemonium. I got his voice mailbox. At the beep, I almost shouted, "Lillian is sick, and I've got to go speak! Start praying!"

When it comes to prayer, Bill is an old pro. Before the night was over, the program in Albany had gone smoothly, thanks to a gracious God and an awesome audience; Papoo had applauded Matthew's performance in the school gym; and Lillian's fever had dropped, so she could sleep through the night (at least *someone* did!). In the morning her daddy took her to the pediatrician, who pronounced her completely well, while Mama winged her way home.

In other words, we survived. And, as Dawn from Oregon pointed out, "Reality is always funny eventually."

Dr. Kevin Leman, the author of *Bonkers,* offered this list, in order, of "Six Major Areas of Stress for Women": children, time, husbands, money, housework, and career.[2] Sure enough, in one twenty-four hour period I had experienced stress in all six of those areas and had learned how to spell G-U-I-L-T with even more gusto.

When women have one of "those kind of days," we often wonder how other women seem to manage better than we do. We chastise ourselves for not measuring up to some angelic ideal, based on a mishmash of images from childhood, *The Donna Reed Show,* and home ec class. We think our husbands want us to be Julia Child in the kitchen, Mother Teresa at church, and Mae West in the bedroom; that our children expect a cross between Amy Grant and Mary Poppins; and that our employers are counting on Mary Kay Ash at a bargain price. To which we must say, "Ain't no way, baby." We've come a long way, but now it's time to make sure we're going in the right direction.

Performance, Perfection, Permission

Alexander Pope said, "Fools rush in where angels fear to tread." What in the world was he talking about? Angels don't tread, they fly, and who ever heard of a "scaredy angel"? Angels have nothing to fear because they only go where they are sent. Ah . . . there's a lesson in that.

Marybeth Weston said it better: "Fools rush in and get all the best seats." For this season, the best seat is in the back row, where we can sit quietly in the dark and let the past few years of our lives play out on the stage before us: single woman, married woman, working woman, mother woman, friend woman, volunteer woman, widow woman, wonder woman, funny woman. But no "perfect woman," unless we follow Wordsworth's definition of us as "yet a spirit still, and bright, with something of angelic light."[3]

"I try to be perfect—I have a feeling this book will tell me that no one is perfect—not even me!" moaned Martha from Florida.

Let's shoot for perfectly wonderful and leave it at that, joining with Arlette from Pennsylvania in seeking "reassurance that our life journeys are filled with lots of 'practice' sessions!"

Most of us want precisely what Louise from Georgia requested: "Permission to be what I am, without feeling like I'm coming up short." We are "taller" than we think! God gives us permission to be ourselves. In fact, the only way to be certain we are walking in grace is to be our very human, often not very angelic, selves and to lean on God to bridge the gap between human possibility and divine perfection.

More than anything, we want "some indication that I'm not the only woman in this world whose life is upside down," as Cheryl so aptly put it. "Just let me know I'm normal!" Mickey pleaded. "Help me realize there are others like me," wrote Kathleen. I can attest that there are at least eight hundred women who from time to time feel that same isolation, those same shifting priorities, that same lack of balance in their lives.

In forty years I've learned that balance does not mean we are good at everything. It means we do what we do well and get help with the rest. It means we do not make the mistake of lighting the candle at both ends and putting a match to the middle. One of the definitions of balance is "the power or ability to decide."[4] Well, we all have that.

Same Wisdom, Different Century

The saying goes that "practice doesn't make perfect, it makes permanent." So, as we mend our wings and plot our course for beyond 2000, it would seem wise to choose carefully not only our destination but also the road map we use for directions. Barbara Walters cautioned, "Whenever there are the kinds of choices there are today, unless you have some solid base, life can be frightening."[5]

Our solid base for this journey together is an ancient manuscript from two millennia ago, known simply as the book of Proverbs. It has thirty-one chapters in all, but we'll focus on the last chapter, a favorite of women through the centuries because it talks about our many roles in life. The experts can't agree on precisely when this section was written—200 B.C., 700 B.C., 950 B.C.—so we'll just call it old wisdom and keep going.

Cervantes said, "A proverb is a short sentence based on long experience." Although Proverbs 31 begins, "The words of King Lemuel" (NKJV), don't be fooled. We're not learning from his experience, we're learning from someone else who'd been around a generation longer, someone who laughed and cried, gave birth and gave advice: his mother.

The full first line says, "The words of King Lemuel, the oracle which his mother taught him" (NASB). This fine son, who is never mentioned by this name anywhere else in the Bible, had the good sense to pay attention when his mother spoke and to write down her words for future generations. As one commentator said, "Mothers, especially queen mothers, were looked upon with great veneration, and treated with marked respect."[6] Those were the good old days.

We know little about this queen mum. Not her name, not her husband's name, not her age, her dress size, nor her target heart range. But we do know two very significant facts:

- She loved God, because the name she chose for her son means "dedicated to God."[7] (I took a page from her book when I named my own long-awaited son "Matthew," which means "gift of God.")

- She loved her son, because she cared enough to teach him not just the ABCs and the 123s but also her values. Jean Fleming, author of *A Mother's Heart,* calls values "an ever present pair of tinted eyeglasses [that] color life for us."[8]

After admonishing her kingly son to stay away from loose women and alcohol (seems to me I mentioned the same thing to Matthew last week!), she encouraged him to speak out for the unfortunate, judge righteously, and defend the rights of the needy. We can almost hear this model mother saying, "Make me proud of you, son!"

But this is all preamble to her real message for Lemuel: how to find a suitable woman with whom to share his life and throne. The twenty-two verses that bring Proverbs to a close are what is known as an acrostic when read in the original Hebrew. Each verse begins with a different letter of the Hebrew alphabet, in order. Just like we might teach a child something important by tying it to A-B-C-D-E, Lemuel's mother followed good oral tradition and sent her son into the world looking for the perfect daughter-in-law, carrying her weighty words with him in his heart.

Onward and Upward

Taunie from Utah expressed her longing for these pages to hold "a balm for the past, encouragement for today, and hope for the future." I can't think of anything better to meet that heartfelt need so many of us share than the wisdom of Proverbs. Although I can't promise to provide what Penny from Alaska requested— "Complete instructions!"—I can help us all focus on *growth,* which is positive, rather than on *improvement,* which suggests that we are something less than fabulous now. We know better.

Each line of the Proverbs poem is different: one paints a humorous word picture, another speaks of deep truths; one may be aimed at the mothers among us, another points to the workplace. That means each chapter will have its own unique tone and direction. Don't let that throw you. Like life itself, this ancient passage travels many roads en route to one destination.

I'll also offer some therapeutic humor, the kind that comes from real life, not joke books. Joyce Kieffer, a women's health professional and treasured friend, described the healing power of laughter divinely: "Laughter is angel music for the soul. We take ourselves too seriously, and laughter gives us wings."

So it is that our journey through the hearts and lives of eight hundred women begins, with frequent stops in Proverbs along the way and a long visit on my own front porch. Stay alert now, because as Richard Purdy Wilbur said, "Outside the open window, the morning air is all awash with angels"!

2
Too Good to Be True

An excellent wife, who can find?

Proverbs 31:10 NASB

Define the Perfect Wife:

Never complains. Is able to leap tall laundry baskets, and is faster than a car pool mom. A chauffeur, who works 40+ hours a week bringing home mega $$. Cooks a huge breakfast and a four-course dinner. Softly reads and puts the children to bed by 8:00, then waits on the sofa in her lingerie ready to please her man all night long. —Alice from Michigan

Ask eight hundred women to define "the perfect wife," and you'll get eight hundred answers with one conclusion: she doesn't exist. Gloria described her as "having no flaws, making no mistakes. There is no such thing!" Susan is sure she is a "nonmortal being that lives in our imagination, setting a standard that is not humanly possible to achieve." Then there's Dauna who wrote, "the definition of a perfect wife eludes me, but I think every woman needs one!"

So, what was Lemuel's mother thinking of, sending him looking for an "excellent" wife? The list of qualities and skills she rattles off for him to look for in a woman is exhausting: self-confident, trustworthy, good with money, devoted to her husband, creative, a gourmet cook, a land developer, strong in character and muscle, sensitive and discerning, hardworking, generous, an expert seamstress, a terrific home decorator, well dressed, self-employed, quick to laugh, never idle, loved by her children, praised by her husband, faithful to God, and well respected by the entire community. LaJoyce Martin, author of *Mother Eve's Garden Club*, says, "She was voted B.C. 1015's top of the top ten. The honor came complete with halo and wings."[1]

"Give me a break!" you say? Happy to. In Jill Briscoe's book *Queen of Hearts*, she refers to this perfect woman of Proverbs 31 as a "Statue of Liberty," which means she is a symbol, larger than life, *not* a real, living, breathing woman who once roamed the earth.[2] One scholar said, "It is a mistake to assume that all the virtues in this section are likely to be embodied in any one woman."[3]

We know. We've tried.

We had some terrific ideas about what constitutes a perfect wife today: "She balances the serious with the humorous, and the responsibilities with the fun," wrote Diana. "Has the ability to meet her spouse's needs because she has met hers first!" were the words of wisdom from Marcia. Rosalind defined the perfect wife as "a woman whose self-confidence is so high she can give freely of her love and talents without doubt, fear, or insecurity."

The proverbial description of womanhood we're about to walk through was meant to be a composite, a "best of" listing. If we made a tally of the finest qualities of each of our ten closest friends, that would most resemble what Lemuel's mother was trying to impress upon her son. Like the '60s song said, "My mama told me . . . you better shop around!"

One Powerful Word

My husband, Bill, "shopped" for me for thirty-four years with the Proverbs 31 description stuffed in his mental back pocket. He had an advantage over most of his fellow shoppers because he knew the original language in which Proverbs was written. We're talking about a man who went to college for twelve years, full time—four years of undergraduate work, eight years at seminary—to earn his Ph.D. in Hebrew. I can imagine what you're thinking: "Say, there's a marketable skill!" Although his current profession as a computer systems specialist does not make much use of those hard-earned credentials, his talents come in handy when studying the Old Testament.

This opening verse about "an excellent wife" has also been translated as "a wife of noble character" (NIV) or, even better, "a capable, intelligent, and virtuous woman" (AMPLIFIED BIBLE). That's us, all right! The Revised Standard Version just says "a good wife." Good grief.

Enter Bill's expertise. It seems the Hebrew word *chayil* that describes this wonder woman is sometimes interpreted as "virtuous" or "excellent" but more commonly means "wealthy, prosperous, valiant, boldly courageous, powerful, mighty warrior." Now, that's a *lot* more than "good"! And the word for *wife,* in Hebrew, *ishshah,* simply means a "mature female." In other words, if you're a single woman, there's something of value for you here too.

I spent nearly five years sitting alone in the pews as a single woman, and the How-to-Be-a-Good-Wife-and-Mother sermons grew . . . tiresome. I knew they were truthful and wise, they just didn't apply to me at that point in my life. The first time I heard this Proverbs 31 passage, I mentally checked out after the opening line, "an excellent wife." Not for me.

Then came the verse about her marketplace skills and entrepreneurial abilities and my ears perked up. Something for never-married, career-driven me after all? Finally, the point of the passage dawned on me: these were the qualities of a virtuous and valiant *single* woman, a woman considered worthy of praise for who she was, not for whom she might marry. The kind of woman who brought tons of talent and crateloads of character to the bargaining table. A woman who was, therefore, an excellent choice for a wife because of the full life she was already leading in her singleness.

It seems this passage was for me after all.

What about the Perfect Husband?

If you're beginning to chafe at the thought of a shopping list for an excellent wife but not for an excellent husband, I understand. Personally, I've always wanted a Proverbs 32 chapter for the guys, something nice and succinct to wave in their faces on Father's Day. As Carol from Texas said when asked to define the perfect wife, "It's the same as 'the perfect husband.' Why should it be different?"

Don't worry, there are plenty of verses throughout Scripture telling men how to be a good husband. Two of my favorite commandments are: "Husbands, love your wives" (Eph. 5:25 NKJV) and "Rejoice with the wife of your youth" (Prov. 5:18 NKJV). Unfortunately for us, these directives are scattered throughout the Bible and harder to point to in a hurry, but they're there. We'll offer our numerous definitions of perfect husbandhood in Chapter 21 and see how our own men "measure up."

Meanwhile, Marilyn knows how the perfect wife might be defined from the man's point of view: "Never says no. Doesn't like to go out to eat. Doesn't like to shop." Rose thinks men want a woman who "earns in the six-figure range and loves football." (I may never earn in the six-figure range, but over the years I've had a six-figure wardrobe: Small, Medium, Large, Extra Large, Queen Size, and Never Mind!)

Some of us think our husbands were hoping for a wife like Donna Reed who, according to Debby, "cooks, cleans, volunteers, supports her husband and kids through every crisis, and does it all in a dress and heels!" And wearing pearls, too, I might add. Mary from Indiana sees *herself* as the perfect wife (good for her!), noting, "We've been working on this arrangement for twenty-nine years to perfect it!"

In all, my eight hundred surveys produced eight hundred different responses, but one pattern became clear: we expect more of ourselves than any one woman could possibly deliver and more than any one husband would honestly want. In response to the survey question, "As a wife, how do you measure up to your own standards?" we gave ourselves a 6.8 as wives, compared to the 7.4 we gave our husbands. But that doesn't tell the whole story. Twenty percent of us awarded ourselves a *higher* rating than we awarded our husbands (knowing full well they would never see the survey!).

Laughing Aloud Allowed . . . and Encouraged

On one thing we agreed: The perfect wife needs to have a strong sense of humor. Donna listed "sensitive, humorous, loving. Also romantic and can stand snoring." Judith knew we'd need "a sense of humor and adventure when slogging through the drudge." And Kay from Iowa insists that when it comes to the perfect wife, there's "no such person—but it's fun to try, laugh at ourselves, and know someone loves us no matter what."

I take great solace in those two areas—laughing at myself and knowing someone loves me—when I remember a particular incident a few springs ago. I was to present an after-dinner program here in Louisville, and Bill was able to join me, a real treat. They seated us at the head table and put me in my customary spot right next to the lectern.

Here's how this usually works: dessert is served and immediately the meeting planner leans over to me and says, "Why don't you go ahead and start your program?" When I stand up to begin, I can see out of the corner of my eye that my dessert is melting into oblivion. Soon, they clear it away, and it's gone forever.

So that night when they put dessert in front of me, I grabbed my spoon and—woosh!—it was history. Thank goodness it was chocolate mousse—I barely needed my teeth. As I looked around the room, I noticed that at most of the tables, dessert hadn't even been served yet. *Good,* I thought, *I'll have enough time to dash off to the ladies' room and get my act together before I speak.* Whispering, "I'll be right back" into Bill's ear, I slipped out of the auditorium and headed for the door marked *Women.*

It was a little "one-seater." Just a toilet, a small sink with a mirror, and a locking door. I pushed in the button to lock the door, stepped up to the mirror, and put on a new layer of Chili Pepper Red lipstick. After fluffing my hair and pinching my cheeks (if it's good enough for Scarlett, it's good enough for me), I sat down to "take care of business," as my mother would say.

While seated, I glanced at my nails. I usually wear a bright red polish to match my lipstick, and my hands look great the day I put it on. But, let a couple of days go by, and I look like a hussy—the ends get all worn and big hunks fall off. Sure enough, that night I realized *I had hussy nails!* I don't know how I'd gotten out of the house with my polish in such bad shape, but there was no question that I would have to do something about it right then and there. No way was I going to stand in front of an audience looking so "unpolished."

I got out my bottle of Daytona Red, which I always carry with me for emergencies, and quickly put on a top coat. I'm an old pro at this, and it didn't take me more than sixty seconds to do both hands. What an improvement!

Then I looked down and felt the color leave my face. My pantyhose were around my ankles.

I was in deep trouble. There are only so many things one can do with wet nails, and pulling up your pantyhose is not one of them. Oh sure, you can wave at a friend or make a phone call—if you have a pencil to push the buttons. And you can drive a car; we've all seen women at red lights with their fingers carefully spread across the top of the steering wheel. Sure, you can drive with a fresh manicure.

But you cannot pull up your pantyhose with wet nails. You'll ruin the polish for sure, or you could get *stuck* there. I was now on full-tilt panic, imagining my client stepping to the lectern any minute to introduce me: "Our speaker tonight . . . ," while the speaker was sitting on the commode with wet nails and pantyhose around her ankles. Help!

It was at that moment of panic that I looked across the ladies' room and saw the hand dryer. *That's it!* I thought, as I struggled to my feet and shuffled over to the metal dryer on the wall. Starting the thing with my elbow, I parked my nails underneath it and thought, *I'll be out of here in a flash!* My manicurist has since explained to me that I was doing the worst possible thing to my nails. The heat actually melts the polish and keeps it sticky.

There I was, cooking my nails. Those dryers are really loud, so it wasn't until it shut off that I realized someone was pounding on the door. It was Bill. "Honey, you're on! You're on! Get out here! Get out here!" he shouted, desperation in his voice.

A plan began to formulate in my mind. "B-i-i-l-lll . . ." I sang out slowly, turning toward the door. "Could you step in here for a minute?"

"Do *what?*" came his muffled reply.

"Don't worry, it's just us, just a one-seater, just a minute!" I said with assurance, doing a tricky side-step toward the door.

I released the button lock and in came Bill, looking wide-eyed. After all, he'd led a pretty sheltered life in seminary and hadn't spent a lot of time in women's rest rooms. He didn't know what he was going to find. What he found, of course, was me. He looked at my face. He looked at my feet. He looked at my face again, and assessed the situation correctly.

"I'm going to have to pull them up, aren't I?" he asked with a groan, as his pivotal role in this unfolding saga became very clear.

And so he began tugging. Our half dozen years of marriage were paying off because soon Bill got the hang of it. All was going well until he hit the control top part. Let's face it, every woman of any size has her own little dance routine about this point, right down to the last kick. But Bill did not know the steps to my dance. I was wiggling; he was waggling. We couldn't get it together, so I started shouting out orders. "No! No! Pull here, do this, try that!"

We were so serious, and the situation so intense, until suddenly I had what you'd have to call an "out of body" experience: I mentally floated above this scene, saw how ridiculous it all was, and exploded with laughter. Sweet Bill, who had been waiting seven minutes to have permission to laugh, was now in hysterics. That just made me laugh harder. And now we were nonfunctional. We couldn't do anything right. We laughed so hard that our muscles were in a complete state of relaxation and therefore useless.

We were soon laughing *so* hysterically that we ceased making any noise at all. Just occasional wheezing sounds. That was when we heard a timid knocking at the door, and the voice of the woman who hired me: "Are you . . . through yet?" she asked faintly. Without even thinking about how this might sound to her, we called out in unison, "Just a minute!"

In Search of a Role Model

One thing is certain: King Lemuel's mom did *not* expect an

excellent woman to wear panty hose! She *did* say of her prospective daughter-in-law: "who can find?" Such powerful, noble, courageous, mighty warrior women *are* hard to find! We don't stand on street corners with a big V on our chest for "virtuous." We're busy accomplishing capable, intelligent, valiant deeds, just like our Proverbs 31 sister. LaJoyce Martin wrote of her, "All of us need an ideal and a heroine. She is our mentor, our sampler."[4]

An excellent wife, who can find?

Near the end of my survey, I posed the question, "Who serves as a role model for you . . . and why?" Of those who responded, nearly 10 percent specifically wrote "none" in all three categories—professional life, family life, spiritual life. It isn't that we don't want role models—we are desperate for them. But everywhere we look are people who disappoint us, people who keep lowering their own standards, people who teach us more about how *not* to act than how to act.

That's why this excellent woman in Proverbs 31 is so appealing to me. She has withstood the test of time, wrinkle free. Her truths are eternal, and her wisdom spans the ages. She is not perfect, but she is excellent. And, above all, she has a sense of humor! In the pages that follow, we'll discover together how her life speaks to us in these last years of the twentieth century. And remember . . . no tips, no hints, no to do lists.

Jean Ann from Utah was describing her vision of the perfect wife, but in truth, it fits our proverbial role model like a glove:

> Honest with herself and others. Takes care of her needs, sets boundaries, nurtures herself, knows she is wondrously made and precious in God's sight. Has a sense of humor, adventure, and love. Has an inner peace, serenity, and joy.

Now that's the kind of excellence I could aspire to!

3

The Six Million Dollar Woman

For her worth is far above jewels.
Proverbs 31:10b NASB

The very idea that the angelic woman of Proverbs 31 had great worth—in the Hebrew: "value, merchandise, or price"—was an incredible statement for that time and place when women were worth little more than cattle and were never worth as much as men. There it is, as bold as you please in Leviticus 27:3–4: the value of a male slave was fifty shekels; the value of a female, thirty shekels. The equal-pay-for-equal-work struggle goes w-a-y back.

Not all women have a lower price tag attached. Robert Redford was willing to pay Demi Moore a cool million for one night of silver-screen romance. It was indeed an *Indecent Proposal,* yet the movie brings to mind an old story about a man who offered a woman a million dollars if she would spend the night with him. "A million dollars?!" she gasped, then added, "well . . . yes, I guess I will." "How about fifty dollars?" he asked. "Sir!" she retorted, "what kind of woman do you think I am?" "Oh, we've already established that," he assured her, "now we're just talking price." Hm-m-m.

The "Looking Good" Route to Self-Worth

For many of us, our worth is tightly wound around some kind of earthly measurement rather than a heavenly one. Sometimes they are very specific measurements. Becky thought the perfect wife would be "36-24-36"; Gail described her as, "Size 6, exercises three times a week." Molly was sure Ms. Perfect would "never have a 'bad hair' day," and Linda described her as "Sophia Loren at dusk."

What do we think would please our husbands in the appearance department? Some women decided it revolved around clothing: "Dressed sexy," said Linda; "Never wore clothes at home," suggested Sara. Vicki thought her mate would be thrilled if "I flattened my tummy or won the lottery!" Well, at least she has a choice, though the odds of either one happening are slim! The dangers of wrapping your self-worth around your physical appearance were addressed at length in my book, *"One Size Fits All" and Other Fables,* so I'll not cover the same ground here. Suffice it to say that if we measure our value by anything so temporal as the smoothness of our skin, the tightness of our tummy, or the size of our thighs, we'll be spending a great deal of money and time on something that will cease to matter once we're put in a pine box, if not sooner.

No one begins a eulogy for the dearly departed by saying, "She was so faithful to her aerobics classes, skipped desserts every chance she got, and maintained a Size 8 figure throughout her marriage." Get real. It's the example we set, the character we demonstrate, and the love we instill in others that will contribute to our sense of worth now and to our sense of contributing to future generations when we've gone on to glory. Luci Swindoll says, "When you love yourself and accept yourself for who you are, you have nothing left to prove."[1]

If self-worth were measured by the inch, Michelle from Ohio, at 6 feet in height, would rise head and shoulders above many of us. After being involved in a minor car accident she said, "I realized my neck was sore and I was dizzy, so the officer called for an ambulance. They arrived, put me on the stretcher, and loaded me into the ambulance. The next thing I heard was the driver saying, 'Could you pull her up? I can't close the door—her feet are sticking out.' This one comment got me through all the whiplash pain, as I imagined what we would have looked like, careening down the street with the doors flapping open, like something from the Keystone Cops!"

If self-worth were measured by the pound, Janet from Virginia's "plus-size personality" would be worth its weight in gold. "One winter, three coworkers and I decided we wanted 'beach bods' by the summer," she wrote, "and we agreed that Weight Watchers was the answer to our dilemma. At the time, Weight Watchers was having their meetings at our local Holiday Inn. We figured we'd visit their All-You-Can-Eat buffet before going to the meeting. [Makes sense to me!]

"We entered the lobby, and I walked up to the desk clerk and said, 'Excuse me.' He turned, took one look at us, and said, 'Upstairs, first door to the left.' I gave him a startled look and replied, 'Pardon me?!' He said, 'You're here for Weight Watchers, aren't you?' I responded in a huff, 'No, we're not. We're a wrestling tag team and were interested in a room, but after that comment, we'll go elsewhere!' and promptly walked out."

And had a good laugh, I'm sure.

When it comes to her sense of worth, an excellent woman is much more than the sum of her parts. For our value to be "far above jewels," it must be far above dress racks, diet clubs, and beauty salons as well.

The "Credentials after Your Name/Money in the Bank" Route to Self-Worth

Some women use other means of measuring worth numerically: in dollars and cents and/or by the number of letters after their names. Few of us, including me, escape the allure of degrees, awards, titles, and other credentials that the world esteems.

For years, when the only letters after my name were the three I'm most proud of—MOM—I still tried to prove my worth using an old-fashioned method: money. I would never have told a soul my dress size, but I'd find some way to hint at my annual earnings at the drop of a hat. Tacky, Liz.

It's been said that "The real measure of our wealth is how much we would be worth if we lost all our money." No doubt about it, many of us seem to confuse net worth with self-worth. As Paula Rinehart, author of *Perfect Every Time*, put it, "[Our] fragile sense of worth is directly attached to abilities and achievements."[2]

These days, it's letters I'm after. In the speaking profession, we have an earned designation called CSP, for Certified Speaking Professional. It takes five years to earn, requires 250 paid presentations for at least 100 different clients, twenty referral letters . . . oh, the list goes on and on.

I couldn't wait to earn my CSP. Because it would mean more income for my family budget? No. Because it would increase my speaking opportunities? Not really. Because it would make me a better speaker, a better servant to my audiences? Not likely. I wanted those three letters after my name so I would be viewed as *somebody* among my professional peers and would impress my clients and audiences. There, I've said it. It looks as bad in print as it feels in my heart.

This is not to say that letters after our names are inherently bad. By no means. I just know that my motives are often not very pure. It's another way to silently say, "I'm better than you." To help me *not* have that attitude when I use those respected letters, I'm going to mentally remind myself of what my real goals are as a CSP: to be Caring, Serving, Purposeful.

I have so much respect for my highly educated husband who is very quiet about his hard-earned letters, Ph.D., and is almost embarrassed when someone calls him Dr. Higgs. His humility speaks volumes to me.

For a man so humble about his own talents, it must be a nuisance to be married to a woman so vocal with her own, especially one who is in the public eye. For example, Bill regularly donates blood to the American Red Cross. One afternoon, sitting in the donor chair, he waited patiently while the nurse checked his temperature, blood pressure, and so forth before she launched into the usual battery of questions.

"Mr. Higgs, have you ever shot up illegal drugs by needle, even once?" Bill shook his head. "Tested positive for the AIDS virus?" "No," he replied as she continued. "Have you been given money or drugs for sex anytime since 1977? Had sex even once with a man? Had sex with a female prostitute?" "No," he assured her, "none of the above!"

As she began swabbing his arm, the nurse asked tentatively, "Uh . . . are you married to Liz Curtis Higgs?" "Yes," Bill responded. She was elated and said, "Oh, I was going to ask you earlier, but I didn't want to get too personal!"

The "Aren't My Children Adorable?" Route to Self-Worth

The best thing I ever did for my husband was give him children. Although there are times when their whining makes his hair (what's left of it) stand up on end, on the whole, he is a model father. Lillian especially knows just how to melt his heart. Sometimes when she sweetly asks him to do something for her, he looks over at me and draws an invisible string around his little finger because that's exactly where she has him wrapped . . . right around her little finger! I can just imagine her saying what Rita from Pennsylvania's daughter did when she came upon her father, fast asleep and snoring loudly. She opened her two-year-old eyes wide with awe and said, "Mommy, listen to Daddy purring!"

Without question, our children can boost our self-esteem. Matthew's first grade class made Mother's Day cards that had a fill-in-the-blank format. I saved mine (of course): "My Mom is smart! She even knows <u>math.</u> I like to make her smile by <u>letting her throw me on the couch.</u>" (Don't get the wrong idea, he likes this!) "My Mom is special because <u>she's in *Today's Christian Woman* magazine.</u>" And, finally, "My Mom is as pretty as a <u>Jewel Sapphire.</u>" What do you know . . . maybe my worth really is "far above jewels!"

But what children give, they can take away. Quickly. Susan from North Dakota remembers her first Sunday at a new church. When she and her family rose for the opening hymn, her daughter whispered none too softly, "Oh, Mommy, don't sing! It's too hard for you!"

My ability to produce two stellar kids for my parents and in-laws to fuss over definitely adds to my sense of value. When Matthew was born, we proudly purchased for Bill's parents (first-timers) one of those bumper stickers that says, "Ask Me About My Grandchildren." Out of a sense of honesty (or maybe a lack of faith in my fertility!) they cut off the last three letters, so it just read "Grandchild." Harrumph! When Miss Lillian showed up twenty months later, we made them scrape off the old sticker and put on a new, plural one.

For her worth is far above jewels.

Is my pride in birthing two beautiful babies a bad thing? Well, not as long as I acknowledge what a gift from God children are and that it is his goodness, not mine, that breathed life into their forms. Those among us who are unable to conceive or cannot bear children can feel incredibly deficient as women, even though we have no control over how our bodies are made and little control over how they work. Yet, "a malfunctioning reproductive system is a threat to self-esteem in a way that a failed kidney or a collapsed lung can never be."[3]

Although we no longer use words like *barren* or *cursed*, the childless woman who longs to bear children can feel like those old labels still fit. Should that be you, seek the encouragement and understanding that only another woman in the very same shoes can provide. And please forgive the insensitivity and foolishness of those of us with kids. Since we've not walked your path of pain, we often put our feet firmly in our mouths.

For those of us with children, we are called to strike a fine balance between experiencing pride and joy in their existence, and drawing too much of our own self-esteem from their accomplishments. I like Bernie from Pennsylvania's view of the balanced woman as one "who puts her family first without putting herself last."

Model Moms

One of the reasons that the job of mother is valued by so many of us is because of the important place our own mothers had in our lives. Of the hundreds who answered the question, "Who serves as a role model for you in your family life?" more than two hundred of us listed our mothers. Christine remembers, "She raised five children alone and instilled a wonderful set of values and confidence in all." Mary acknowledged that her mom "has lived through much in her life and still finds beauty and laughter—at eighty she is still learning, bowling, cooking, and volunteering!" Our mothers didn't have to be flawless to earn our respect. Shirley wrote, "She was not a perfect mom, so I can learn from her mistakes."

Then there's this story from Cathy in Kentucky. She spent Mother's Day 1993 with her own mother first and then with her husband's mother. After a long day of meals and gifts, they finally walked in the door of their home and parked their eight-month-old son on the kitchen floor. While she and her husband were carrying things in from the car, the baby found the telephone, started playing with it, and hit the redial button. Of course, they didn't know that . . . yet.

Cathy's husband remarked that he thought the day went well. Cathy did not agree. "I rarely lose my temper, but this time I started into him. We had given his mother a $75 gift, and I told him we were never going to spend that much money again because she never thanked us, never commented whether she liked it, just opened her gift and went on. I must have ranted and raved about this for fifteen minutes.

"About then, I asked my husband if he had seen the Barney bag, because it had my aspirin in it and at this point I definitely needed some aspirin. 'You must have left it at your mother's,' he said, so I jumped in the car and drove the ten minutes it takes to get there.

"My mother greeted me at the door and asked me if I'd come for the Barney bag. 'Oh, did you find it?' I asked. 'No,' she said, 'I just heard about it.'" Literally.

It seems that when their son hit redial on the phone, he'd reached her mother, who had listened in on the whole conversation. "We laughed and laughed," Cathy said, "but were *very* grateful he'd called my mother and not my mother-in-law!" Too close for comfort, that one. A sitcom in the making.

The "I Can Do It All" Route to Self-Worth

Judy from Massachusetts had one request for this book: "Convince me that most people don't really do everything naturally with no effort." Like the duck who appears to glide serenely on the lake while paddling like mad to stay afloat, many of us make the "I-can-do-it-all" approach to life look easy—while we put in twenty-hour days to pull it off.

Workaholism and its twin, perfectionism, are an increasing problem as we rush toward the new millennium. Paula Rinehart wrote, "Our culture seems increasingly geared to let such excesses masquerade as virtues."[4] Working mothers are especially good at playing the "my stress is bigger than your stress" game as we compare calendars like grandmothers compare photo brag books: "Mine has more in it than yours!"

A dear friend in my profession described her urge to put too much on her calendar: "I discovered that it had little to do with financial need. It was an inner drive that pushed me to *do,* to *perform,* to *have,* to *show that I could do it!* All wrapped up with self-esteem issues. It was a very lonely realization." Now she has posted next to her phone a copy of one crazy month's schedule from a few years back with a banner headline at the top: *"Never again! Say no!"*

Sometimes I look at my speaking calendar and cry. The tears well up from two sources: gratitude for the opportunities *and* concern for my ability to pull it all off. Believe me, I love making audiences laugh and making clients happy. But sometimes, it comes at the cost of my own laughter and my own happiness. Not to mention my family's joy and contentment. Ugh.

Very slowly, I am learning that not only is it okay not to "do it all," it's dangerous to try.

Some of us even wrap our self-worth around service to the church, thinking, "If it's for God, it must be worthwhile; therefore, I am worthwhile too!" Peg Rankin, in *How to Care for the Whole World and Still Take Care of Yourself,* listed some of the seductive messages we hear concerning our spiritual areas of service:

- Take on more than you can handle. You can never do enough for God.

- Set goals and push yourself to achieve them. You want to hear "well done" on Judgment Day.

- Gauge the effectiveness of your service by concrete evidence. If you don't see results, there probably aren't any.[5]

Ouch! These hit too close to home for this woman, especially that last one about looking for tangible, measurable results. It's hard for me to remember that, in matters of faith, invisible growth is the best kind.

Enough Is Enough

Carol from Maryland expressed her need to know "how to recognize enough is enough." *Enough* for me now means quitting an activity *before* it hurts me emotionally, physically, or spiritually. *Enough* means getting my needs met elsewhere, so I'm not looking for self-worth in inappropriate places, such as my to do list. *Enough* means asking for help from a therapist, a friend, a mate, a child, a minister, or—best of all—from God himself. *Enough* means sanity, serenity, and sincerity. *No* still works, if we mean it.

For our worth to be "far above jewels," we must set our price so high that we cannot be bought—not for beauty, money, fame, or letters after our names. Then, when we give ourselves to those whom we love most, we are opening up a treasure chest and not an empty box.

4

Trust Me!

The heart of her husband safely trusts her.

Proverbs 31:11 NKJV

*I*t took me nearly thirty-two years to find a man who trusted me with all his heart, in part because most of the men I met *I* wouldn't trust, not even with my cat, let alone my emotions.

Despite the carefree, glamorous picture the media paints of singleness, most of us who've been there know the truth: it can be tough to be single, especially if you're over thirty, and even more so if you've never been hitched. I remember somewhere near my thirty-first birthday having dinner at a local restaurant with five other never-married friends and laughing hysterically at the thought of all our biological clocks, loudly ticking away in that crowded booth. The more we thought about it, the harder we howled.

Your married friends don't find singleness funny, they find it . . . sad. "Seeing anyone?" they'll ask tentatively, pity in their eyes. When you say, "Not right now," the look on their faces is, "Awwwww, poor thing!"

The assumption of married people is that single people are on constant alert for a possible mate. The truth is, single women have good days and bad days. Days when you are so thankful to be enjoying your singular existence that the very concept of a man cluttering up your apartment and your life would be unthinkable. Then there are those other days, lonely days, when the thought of having a nice, warm fella to curl up with to watch an old movie sounds like nirvana.

"At forty-four, I feel I have found Mr. Close—I'm old enough to know he's not perfect!" wrote Charlotte from Oklahoma. Some of us would be happy with a Mr. Close, and others of us aren't even interested in a Mr. Perfect. One of the questions included in the survey was, "If you are not married now, how important is having a husband to you and why?" On a scale of one to ten, the 136 single women who responded were ambivalent about wanting a husband. Their responses averaged 5.4, but nearly a third gathered toward the No Thanks end of the scale, and exactly the same number—28 percent—leaned toward the Now, Please side of things.

The less-than-enthusiastic crowd had some very good reasons for their choices: "I believe that it is possible to be a whole, happy, fulfilled person without being married, and right now I am one," said Kim from Florida. Barbara from Kentucky wrote, "I'm emotionally still defining what my needs are, so finding someone compatible will have to come after I've completed this process." "The men in my life cost me both financially and emotionally and I feel I'm better off without a man. All they're good for is lifting heavy things," responded Nancy from North Dakota.

Oh, men have a couple of good qualities beyond heavy lifting, but there are few women alive who haven't shared those same feelings about the male of the species at one point or another. Dauna's sage advice is, "If your husband leaves you and it teaches you to never trust or love again, then you've lost much more than a husband."

Some women longed to be married enough to circle Now, Please! They have their own reasons for wanting a partner ASAP:

"I think life is hard to do alone! Would be great to have a kindred spirit around the house."

Patt from Minnesota

"Someone to laugh with, wake up with, make *me* breakfast in bed and share life with."

Martha from Florida

"I am tired of dating. I go out with too many boyfriends and I call them by the wrong names. Disaster!"

Gloria from Washington

Gee, my dating life never got that crazy! If anything, I kept calling them by my cat's name. (Just FYI, men don't react well to being called Big Cat.)

Sometimes our lives are already very full, and there isn't much room or time or need for marriage. Sandra from Wisconsin wrote, "I have freedom, a good job, make my own decisions, am busy and active, have a variety of friends and great support from other women and my grown children. Frankly, I'm not sure I have much left to give to another relationship in my life."

Finally, sitting in the middle of the No Thanks and Now, Please crowds is Linda from Missouri, whose balanced response may come from some hard-won experience: "With the right person, having a husband can be heaven on earth. The wrong person can destroy your entire essence as a person."

Eight Winning Traits

I am fortunate to have chosen the right person. But I believe strongly you have to *be* the right person yourself, first. God in his wisdom did not bring Bill and me together until we were older, wiser, and had a handle on the stuff that really matters. I definitely needed time to work on being the kind of woman who would thrill the heart of the first-class kind of guy I wanted. In other words, I made a list of the qualities I was looking for in a man, then set out to develop them in myself. That way, if I didn't end up finding a good man, I could still be an "excellent woman!"

Here's my list, taken in part from Proverbs 31 and included in our survey:

Flexibility	Creativity
Trustworthiness	Focus
Generosity	Organization
Confidence	Joyfulness

I asked eight hundred women, "How would you rank these, in order of importance to you today?" So now I'll ask you to do the same. Which would be number one for you? Number two? Number three, and so on?

More than one woman jotted a note in the margin, saying "This is hard!" or "They're all important!" Exactly so. Ranked on a scale of one to eight, one being the highest, here's how we stacked them:

1. Trustworthiness

2. Joyfulness

3. Confidence

4. Flexibility

5. Generosity

6. Organization

7. Creativity

8. Focus

Trustworthiness was markedly higher than its nearest competitor, joyfulness (which I expected to come in first!). Lemuel's mother would've agreed with our assessment, which is why she pointed her son toward finding a trustworthy mate. My sense is that the kind of man we want to share our lives with today would also rank the above qualities in much the same way. Thousands of years later, good stuff is still . . . good stuff.

Here Comes the Groom

Not to sound sappy, but my dear Bill truly has those eight traits, and about in that order. (Okay, organization might be shaky.) People always ask me, "Where did you meet such a great guy?" We met at a wedding. Not our own. I mean we had a short courtship, but not that short.

This particular wedding united two friends of mine (and of Bill's, I would find out later). The groom worked in radio and knew us both; the bride was a member of my church, which is where the wedding took place.

As a never-married, over-thirty woman, I didn't care for weddings. No, it was stronger than that. I *hated* weddings. I would sit in the pew, watching the church fill up like the loading of the ark—two by two—all the while moaning under my breath, "Where's *mine?*"

The woman getting married was named Liz, which meant the whole time she was taking her vows, I took them with her. You know, just in case I never got to actually say them myself *or* as a means of practice, if someday I did marry. When the ceremony concluded, I noticed a handsome, smiling man about two rows back, all by himself. No ring on his left hand. Hm-m-m. I knew vaguely that he worked at the radio station with Doug, the groom, but little else. Determined to learn more, I headed in his direction, thinking, *Well, I can at least say "hello"!*

So, I did. And he did. Nice smile, warm handshake. Then he asked me, "What is that sculpture up in front of the church?" That sculpture was a very free-form artistic interpretation of a cross, not an unusual thing to have in front of a church. But then it suddenly struck me: *This guy may not go to church. He may not know what a cross is. Hey, he may not know who God is! Maybe I ought to introduce the two of them.* Off I went, describing the cross itself, repentance, baptism, Acts 2:38, regeneration, everything this guy needed to know.

I went on and on, as only I can, while he was smiling and nodding and smiling and nodding. *I've got a live one here!* I thought to myself. Then slowing down to catch my breath, I said, "So, tell me a little about yourself."

"Well . . ." he said slowly, "I'm an ordained minister."

I was speechless. (This is rare.) "A minister?" I finally said, as a smile slid up one side of his face. "No kidding!" I stammered. "Did I get everything right?"

"You did well," he assured me, and we both laughed.

One thing Bill found out about me right away was that I cared more about his relationship with God than any potential relationship with me. And that was exactly what attracted him to me. That, and my level of self-acceptance. And my laugh!

We stood there and talked in the sanctuary until it was empty, and I realized I didn't have the faintest idea where the wedding reception was. Bill had saved the directions and said, "Why don't you follow me?" Happy to.

At the reception, we kept an eye on each other as we mingled around the room, finally ending up at the same table. (Imagine that.) More talking, more sharing, then finally we exchanged business cards, and I said, "Call me sometime."

Now came the Big Wait. Four or five days later (not wanting to appear overanxious, he said), Bill called. I wasn't home, but my answering machine was. I can still remember coming in and finding the usual 0 replaced with a 1. For a single woman who had not dated in years, any night without a goose egg on the machine was a good night!

The message was short and sweet. A warm voice with a Kentucky twang said, "I wondered if you might like to go to dinner sometime next week?" I might. "Please give me a call back, Liz," were his final words. Not wanting to appear overanxious either, I waited four or five seconds before dialing his number.

Our first date came two weeks later; our wedding date was exactly eight months after that. (The only reason we waited that long is it takes a while to special order a custom-built Size 20 wedding gown!) We'll be forever grateful to Liz and Doug for inviting both of us to their wedding, never dreaming that one ceremony would lead to another.

On Bended Knee

For Linda from Indiana, that first meeting with her future husband was even more unusual than our ceremonial one. "One of the guys on my bowling team, Bob, asked me if I'd like to go on a blind date with his brother. I said okay, and he gave his brother my phone number. This guy called and we went on a date.

"During the evening, I asked him why he and his brother were both named Bob. He said he didn't have a brother named Bob. Getting suspicious, I asked him where he got my phone number. 'From Stan.' 'Who's Stan?' I asked. 'I thought Stan was *your* brother,' he said.

"It turned out that Stan was the first Bob's brother, who really didn't want to go out on a blind date, so he passed my number along to Bob number 2. I guess it was meant to be, because the second Bob is my husband!"

It's fun to hear not only how people met, but also where the proposal actually occurred. Pat from Michigan received her proposal of marriage in the shirt aisle at a Target store. Her husband-to-be was down on his knees supposedly looking for a shirt in his size and said, "Pat, come here, I've found one." As she rounded the corner, he put his hands together and said, "Honey, will you marry me?" Her response, of course, was: "You crazy nut!"

The heart of her husband safely trusts her.

Dearly Beloved

Let's face it: you can fall in love, but you can't fall in trust. Trust doesn't come from romantic dinners and kisses on the doorstep. Trust, unlike love, is not blind. Trust is based on time, experience, and year-in, year-out faithfulness. It takes a few turns of the calendar before "her husband has full confidence in her" (NIV).

My own trust in Bill had to grow quickly after our short eight-month courtship, especially after we had the rolls of film developed from our honeymoon. The first photos, taken a few months before we met, featured Bill with his arm around another woman! You should've seen his face when I pulled out those photos. . .

After nearly a decade, I can say with assurance that we trust each other completely. He trusts me with our money, the mutual care of our children, and all our possessions, even the riding lawn mower and the remote control. Most of all, he trusts me with his *heart,* his emotional center, even though, as his best friend these many years, I know all his tender spots, pressure points, and fault lines.

Of course, the reason mutual trust works so well is because our men have plenty of dirt on us too. When I asked women to finish the sentence, "My husband would be so proud of me if I . . . ," Lynne said, "was always ready to go fifteen minutes before he is"; "arrived home when I said I would," thought Laurie; "parked the car straight in the garage," guessed Laura, and Doris was certain of this: "got caught up—just once!"

Rosita Perez, a wonderful speaker and friend from Florida, tells a story that has a very familiar ring to it.

> One morning I baked a two-layer cake, frosted with chocolate, intending to serve it that night for dessert. I wanted to taste a little bit to see if it was moist enough. It was. It was delicious. So I took another sliver. The sliver became a slab. I ended up cutting a two-inch channel right in the center of the cake, all the way across. Then I could put the two sides together and refrost it so no one would be the wiser. The problem was, I couldn't stop. I kept putting those sides together all afternoon, and I eventually

ended up with something that was shaped like a very long, very thin football. I couldn't let my husband see what I had done, so I ate the football. When he arrived home from work, I served him his dinner, and he asked, "Aren't you eating?" And I said, with my best Poor Me face, "No-o-o . . . I'm not very hungry."

Bless His Heart

A group of my friends gathered with me to study Proverbs 31 while this book was in progress, and one week I gave them a homework assignment. "Ask your husband, 'What speaks love to you?' Don't worry, he'll know what you mean." They came back with their research, and we found the answers to be very different than we expected. One husband said he sensed her love for him by "the look in your eyes when I enter the room"; another said, "the way you address me in conversation"; a third answered, "the sacrifices you are willing to make on our behalf." With answers like that, it's a question worth asking.

In our marriage, there is a question that Bill poses several times a week. He knows just when I need to hear it, just when my to do list is on tilt, and I'm feeling overwhelmed. He simply says, "What can I do to bless you tonight?" And he means specific tasks, something he could do to make my life easier—the dishes, the laundry, the groceries, whatever. Do I deserve a man this good? Absolutely not. But I don't deserve grace either, and I'm grateful to have that poured over me daily.

Thank you, Lord, for grace. And for Bill. Help me be worthy of his trust and his love.

5

Money Is the Root of All Shopping

He has no lack of honest gain or need of dishonest spoil.
Proverbs 31:11b AMPLIFIED BIBLE

I remember the day Bill told me, wide-eyed with horror, about a friend whose wife would hide her purchases in the trunk, then sneak them into the house when he wasn't there. I tried to appear shocked as I made a mental list of all my friends who had done exactly that. (Is there a woman alive who hasn't, at least once, had to do a two-step when asked by her husband, "Is that a new dress?")

So, how did Bill respond when I asked him about spending money? "Just make sure we can afford it." He doesn't just mean, "Is there enough in our account to cover this?" He means, "Do we really need it? Is it a good value for the price?" and, especially in Bill's case, "Is it marked down 50 percent or more?" He gives *tightwad* a whole new meaning. We're perfectly paired, since I am the very personification of the term *spendthrift*.

"No lack of gain" has nothing to do with putting on weight. It means we don't spend all the household money. (Who says the ancient wisdom of Proverbs isn't right on time for the '90s?) Our surveys indicate that we have a pretty good notion of what our husbands prefer in the area of finances: "Pinch pennies until they scream," wrote Vanessa from Nebraska. "Live within the budget," said Judy from Alabama.

Elma knew what would please her man: "Cut up all my charge cards." For Debbie, he'd be happy if she'd "balance the checkbook more than once a year." And Dawn Marie understood what it would take to really make her husband smile: "Quit spending money, of course!"

If men trust us not only with their hearts, but also with the family checkbook, we "earth angels" owe it to those we love to practice some fiscal responsibility. Because it's literally a dollars and cents issue, sometimes it can be the easiest area of our lives to work on, as opposed to "act more loving" or "don't whine." On the other hand, the whole earning/spending/saving issue is reported to be the single thing married couples argue about the most.

Mean Green

When it comes to cash, there never seems to be enough of it. As Richard Armour said, "That money talks, I'll not deny; I heard it once, it said, 'Good-bye!'" My experience is that when payday comes, the check goes in the bank, the balance looks terrific, I spend twenty minutes writing checks to pay the bills, and the balance is right back where it was when I started. In theory, one would think that if we earned just a little more money, it would solve that problem. My own life tells me that when we make a little more, we spend a little more—sometimes before we even earn it! Elsewhere in Proverbs are these words of wisdom:

> Do not weary yourself to gain wealth,
> Cease from your consideration of it.
> When you set your eyes on it, it is gone.
> For wealth certainly makes itself wings,
> Like an eagle that flies toward the heavens.
>   (Prov. 23:4–5 NASB)

When I asked women to tell me what they wanted more of and less of in their lives, many said, "More money (without being greedy)" and "Less fear of not being able to pay the bills." Maybe Joe E. Lewis was right: "It doesn't matter if you're rich or poor, as long as you've got money."

Bill does better when funds are tight than I do. Like many families, we have a good car and a second car, meaning it has more wear and tear and fewer miles left on it. Poor Bill always gets the second car because I need the more reliable one for longer speaking jaunts. He's always endured the clunker car with a sweet spirit. When I asked him how the current one was holding up, he smiled brightly and said, "I stepped out on faith today and filled the gas tank!"

"How Much Was That Again?"

Since the Proverbs woman was so trustworthy, especially in financial matters, Bill and I agreed from the beginning to stick to a joint checking account and one credit card, and I would carry both the checkbook and credit card in my purse. Uh-oh. The verse clearly says that the husband "lacks nothing of value" (NIV), but Bill was definitely going around empty-handed!

It was hard for both of us to adjust to a two-income, one-checking-account marriage. After being in graduate school for so many years, Bill was used to being broke. After eight years of a successful radio career, I was used to having, and spending, lots of money, no questions asked.

Funny thing about husbands. They ask questions. "What is this credit card slip for? 'Merchandise'? What does that mean?" I would sigh and try to remember what I bought where, and he'd shake his head and grumble. Finally, we agreed that we would tell each other when we were going to buy something. I found it to be a nuisance, but it did keep financial peace in our marriage, so I tried to be very faithful about reporting expenditures.

But there was this one Saturday morning. I did a presentation for a very small group of women at a local church and was surprised and delighted when they generously gave me a check at the end of our time together. Would you not consider that "found money"? The kind that's not in the budget? A gift straight from heaven to your wallet?

Well, I took that nice check, hit the bank machine to cash it, and bought a small cut glass window for our honeymoon home. I almost danced in the door with it, sure Bill would be as pleased as I was. "Did the women of the church give you that?" he asked as soon as he saw the window. "Wel-l-l-l," I began, "sort of!" His face darkened. "What do you mean, 'sort of'?" he wanted to know. "Well," I said, "they gave me a check and this is how I spent it! Isn't it beautiful?"

"Liz!" he said with his I'm-not-happy sigh. "That should have been spent on groceries." I was tempted to make him eat it. "Okay, okay, I'll ask first next time," I assured him, still smarting from his ingratitude over my find. It was days before the glass window was hung because it had caused such a fuss.

As the weeks went by, I did a better job of checking with Bill about this purchase and that. Soon, he began to relax as he understood that I could indeed be trusted, and that there really were sufficient funds on hand to cover a few whimsical acquisitions. Bill, however, still consulted me about every little expense. I remember one day when he called, saying, "I saw this computer magazine while I was out at lunch today. It's $2.95. Do you mind if I buy it?" I'm thinking, *Is this a good time to tell him about the couch?*

Filthy Lucre

Dianna from Oklahoma had a knack for tossing money around too. "One Christmas, while entering the mall, I noticed a lady taking donations for a mission project, using a big red cup. After I finished my shopping, I was leaving the store in a hurry (as usual). I reached into my purse, grabbed some coins, walked up behind the lady with the cup, and dropped it in. Instead of hearing the usual jingle of change hitting metal, I heard a curious 'plop.' I had deposited my money in a stranger's soft drink! I was so embarrassed, I practically ran to my car!" It makes me wonder whether the person (a) finished the soda with the dirty money in it and/or (b) rinsed the coins off and saved them. Speaking of laundering cash, Carole from Utah has managed as many as seventeen different companies at one time and admits, "I need more laughter in my life." Sometimes her own customers provide that opportunity. One day, a woman came into Carole's storage business to pay her rent and proceeded to take off her sock and dump the cash on the counter.

"Oh, I better wash it for you!" she said and headed for the rest room. When she brought the wet money back, Carole's understanding employee simply spread the bills across the radiator to dry. No "lack of honest gain or need of dishonest spoil" there! Just an iron, perhaps.

He has no lack of honest gain or need of dishonest spoil.

Then there was last June, when Bill was giving his brand new riding lawn mower a spin around the property. There he sat looking like Mr. Green Jeans, tooling around the backyard, totally unaware of the disaster that lurked right behind him.

Slowly, his shiny new leather wallet began inching its way out of his back pocket. Every time the mower took a bounce, it sneaked out a little bit more. When Bill hit a gopher hole, the wallet was properly launched while its owner rode on. Moments later he made the turn and drove that shiny new blade right over the top of his wallet full of credit cards, car registrations, a driver's license and other Very Important Papers. Thanks to Bill's miserly ways, there was only one dollar in the billfold.

Of course, he didn't miss his wallet until the next day, after an overnight thunderstorm had put the finishing touches on the scene. We looked in the house, we looked in the car, we even looked in the pockets of all his pants—which is when the horrific possibility dawned on him. Pale around the ears, he headed for the back door, saying, "Let me just check something." He came in moments later with that something in his hands. A stray Chevron here, a partial Sears there, but otherwise it was hard to tell what was what, the cards and papers were so gnarled beyond recognition.

We always handle such disasters by beginning with the phrase, "The good news is . . ." In this case, the good news was: this husband had entrusted his wife with duplicates of all those credit cards, the checkbook, and most of the cash. "The heart of her husband safely trusts her" . . . to keep her wallet safely in her purse.

When I told Bill I planned to share his experience in this book, he said, "No one will believe you."

"Why not?" I whined. "It happened, didn't it?"

"Sure, but it also happened in a TV commercial," he informed me, "and your readers will think you borrowed it."

"Nonsense," I told him, "the commercial people obviously lifted the story from *you!*"

Living on Less

When Bill and I married, we set up housekeeping on a property so small that we didn't even need a lawn mower. Cutting the grass meant a Weed Eater and ten minutes, and you were done. Money was tight in the early years, and on paper there was no way Bill and I could pull off starting a business *and* starting a family, financially.

But we did it. Sometimes it meant borrowing money from a loved one for a season, or paying back our obligations v-e-r-y slowly. Most of the time it meant doing without. Peanut butter was a daily fare (until it got so pricey), and dining out meant we split a Happy Meal at McDonald's, and Matthew got the prize!

For fun, we went for long drives up and down the neighboring streets in the evening while Matthew snoozed in his car seat. As the houses got bigger and more expensive, we would marvel at their size and guess at their value. After a few blocks, my eyes would start gleaming, green with envy. So, to keep our covetousness in check, we would turn down streets where the houses and yards were smaller, the cars at the curb were older, the clothes on the line were more modest.

Finally, we would pull into our own driveway and say, "Oh, what a mansion! Thank you, God, for our beautiful home!" It was more cottage than castle, but it was ours (and the bank's), and we were most grateful. We had no "lack of honest gain" and plenty of unmerited grace.

6

The Best of Intentions

She does him good and not evil.

Proverbs 31:12 NKJV

*O*ne problem here: this verse doesn't leave any room for "she puts up with him!" She not only does NOT do evil, but she does only good things. That's a lot of pressure for us less-than-angelic wives, who try hard but stumble. The Amplified version helps us understand even more clearly that the woman who loves her man "will comfort, encourage and do him only good."

If your reaction is, "How come he doesn't have to be good to ME?!" don't worry. He does. There are plenty of verses that point to the equality of the marriage relationship, the concept of serving one another, belonging to one another, etc. Meanwhile, doing good, and not evil, to the men we love just makes sense.

"Good" and "Evil" and Apples

Matthew learned the difference between doing good rather than evil one fateful day in first grade. On the classroom wall was a large colorful tree with each child's name, written on an apple, hanging from the branches. If a child misbehaved—horrors!— his apple was dropped from the tree and into the basket below, where it stayed until the next day. If the apple stayed in the tree all week, the child was rewarded with a trip to the prize box.

Our mild-mannered Matthew never dropped his apple. Week after week he came home with something from the prize box and a note from his teacher: "Your son is such a nice boy." Music to a mother's ears.

Until the day I picked him up from school, and the first words out of his mouth were, "Mom, I dropped my apple!" I couldn't help it—a tear slid out of the corner of my eye, knowing how disappointed he must be. "I'm sorry, Mom!" he said, shedding a few tears of his own as he clung to my coat.

"I know just what to do," I assured him, wiping away our tears as we headed to the car. "Matthew, before we even drive away, let's tell God what happened. You'll feel much better after we do."

Sitting in the front seat next to me, Matthew bowed his sweet, round, Charlie Brown-shaped head, folded his hands in mine, and waited.

"You have to go first," I whispered.

He took a deep breath and finally said in a voice filled with juvenile emotion, "Oh, God! I'm such a sinner!"

It took everything in me not to burst out laughing. I patted his hand to get my mind off it, as he continued to tell God what a mistake he had made, horsing around when he should've been listening to the teacher.

When he finished, I said, "Son, I have some good news for you! The Bible says that if we confess our mistakes, God is faithful and just to forgive us completely and wash away our sins. That means we never need to talk about this again, because you're forgiven and it's forgotten! Isn't that terrific?"

His eyes, bright with tears, blinked with astonishment. "Really? That's great!" With that, our discussion moved immediately to other things, and no mention of the dropped apple was made again. Later that evening, when Bill got home from work, Matthew brought it up himself, giving his dad the Cliff's Notes version of the story. "But it's okay, Dad," he assured him, winking at me, "Mom knows a great verse!"

Children really do grasp more than we give them credit for

sometimes. Esther from Illinois remembers when her eleven-year-old daughter was sitting with her older siblings watching an educational program about human reproduction. Soon they began to show footage of the sperm joining with the egg and the announcer stated that the sperm actually attacked the egg. When one of her older brothers stated that maybe she was too young to see that part, she replied, "Oh, I know all about that. That's called 'the battle of the sexes'!" Even at a young age, we females know what a challenge it will be to do men "good and not evil"!

"Hold Your Tongue!"

How do we think our husbands would define such "good" treatment? "Quit nagging!" said Sandy. "Quit arguing!" said Debra. Cass knows he would be grateful if she "would be kind to him," or "would learn to go with *his* flow," wrote Sonya from Oklahoma.

For me, if I could hold my tongue now and again, that would be good enough for Bill. Harlan Miller once said that "the difference between a successful marriage and a mediocre one consists of leaving about three or four things a day unsaid."

Bill and I ate at an Italian restaurant recently and, as is their custom, they served his fettuccine with a large spoon. "Gosh, I've never eaten pasta with a spoon!" he said, trying valiantly to scoop up a spoonful of the slippery stuff. Doing my best not to have an air of superiority in my voice, I said, "Honey, the spoon is for twisting the pasta around your fork."

"Huh?" he said, looking puzzled. "Watch," I told him, as I wound my fork around a few strings of spaghetti, then twisted it carefully into the spoon. In an instant, I had a tidy twirl to pop in my mouth, and did so.

"Hey, that really works," he said, stabbing a large hunk of pasta and beginning to spin it into his spoon. But storm clouds were gathering. The already too-large lump began growing like the proverbial rolling stone gathering moss, only in this case, it was gathering fettuccine and clam sauce with alarming speed. Soon, the better part of his entire serving was on the end of that fork and I feared that soon the red-and-white checked tablecloth would be sucked into its vortex.

When he started to aim the huge blob of pasta toward his mouth, I could keep silent no longer. "Down, Bill, down!" I whispered. Even the best men need mothering occasionally.

Sometimes, in trying to do him "good and not evil," we overdo. As a newlywed, Lynnette from Alaska thought she was doing the right thing by giving her husband the nice, brown toast, the just crisp bacon, and the eggs over easy, keeping the burned toast, black bacon, and hard-cooked eggs for herself. "After about three months, he looked at me from across the kitchen table and asked, 'Why do you always keep the good stuff for yourself, and give me the bad stuff?!' I was dumbfounded and assured him 'Not a problem!'" Apparently, "well-done" in his family meant "overdone" in hers!

Speaking of tasty stories, Bill and I did the traditional "keeping of the top of the wedding cake" to enjoy on our first anniversary. As I recall, we both took one bite and threw it away. Yuck! Major freezer burn. But that's not how things turned out at Leslie's house in Utah. She and her husband dressed up in formal attire to enjoy a delicious anniversary dinner together, with the wedding cake top proudly displayed on a beautiful crystal pedestal cake plate.

"When it was time for dessert, my husband very politely said that he really didn't think he could eat any, but he'd support me if I did. The next thing I knew, he dove head first into the cake! When he lifted his face out, his nose and mustache were covered with frosting. I thought we would die laughing . . . remember, we were still in our formal attire. He then began to coax me to do the same thing. As I leaned toward the cake to take a bite, he very gently pushed my head. Talk about frosting up the nose! It wasn't a pretty sight!"

Maybe we also need a verse that says, "he does *her* good, and not evil!"

Who Is in Control Here?

For some reason, when Bill and I have a disagreement, it usually revolves around home remodeling and repairs (or the lack thereof). Cathy from Iowa remembers the time she was less than helpful to her husband: "He was trying to strip the paint on our kitchen woodwork when it caught on fire. I screamed 'FIRE!' ran some water in a bucket, and proceeded to throw it on him. To add insult to injury, he'd already put the fire out himself. That was almost as bad as the time I put his rubber rainsuit in the electric dryer and it melted!"

My Bill is not a sports fanatic or remote control tyrant, but many women have husbands who are both. Harriet from Kentucky described one Sunday afternoon when she was sitting in the living room reading when her husband came in. He flipped on the football game, watched it for a few minutes, turned to her, and said "Would you watch this for me?" and left the house.

Then there was the time Donna from Ohio got to watch an entire show without any channel surfing because her husband had gone to bed early. When it came time to turn off the television, the remote control was nowhere to be found. Not in the kitchen, the bathroom, or in the Lazy Boy. She gave up, turned the set off manually, and crawled into bed. "Honey, have you seen the remote control?" she asked him, yawning. He slid one sleepy arm down to the floor next to the bed and held up the missing control. Apparently he was still in charge of it, even in his sleep!

She Does Him Good and Not Apple Butter . . .

Bev in Indiana remembers an occasion when her own husband was "in the dark."

My daughter and grandson had come over for the day so we could make apple butter together. We spent the day getting the apples prepared and by late afternoon we had a batch simmering on the stove. We'd discussed the need of a chest of drawers for little Ben's room, and I had promised to buy one if we could get it at a decent price. Looking through the paper, we saw one advertised and decided we'd turn the stove off and head to town to check it out.

So with the house in a mess, I flung off my apron and we headed out the door, leaving dirty dishes stacked high and toys everywhere. We didn't rush, enjoying the time together, and stopped for a few groceries on the way home.

When we pulled into the driveway, it was filled with cars. My immediate thought was, 'Oh no, Rod had a meeting scheduled and forgot to tell me!' Then I realized that *I* was the one who had forgotten about my own Ladies Auxiliary meeting. I ran in the house to find seven of my officers sitting around the table with big smiles on their faces.

I soon learned that my husband had been called out of the shower to answer the doorbell. He said, 'Erma stood there like she thought she belonged so I asked her why she was here,' and that's when he found out about the meeting. More folks kept arriving, so they cleaned up the house and got things set up.

It was unreal. Of course, I hadn't prepared refreshments, but I put out some snack mix and fixed glasses of iced tea for everyone. The biggest laugh came when the chairman picked up her Snoopy glass and read: "There's no excuse for not being prepared!"

A Good Man Is a Good Thing

My own husband has the patience of Job. If we're sitting at a red light, and he's behind the wheel, I'm over on the passenger side with a gas pedal of my own. Sure, it's invisible, but I find myself reaching my foot toward it as I crane my neck to the left and right, ready to take off like a shot.

The light changes, and Bill's foot is still on the brake. "Bill, it's green!" I say, assuming he just didn't see it. Still no forward motion. He's looking around, hands on the wheel at 10:00 and 2:00. "Bill, it's green!!" I say with some measure of desperation.

He turns to me and says, "There'll be another one."

I'm the first to admit that I often have a little fun at Bill's expense, but there are two important considerations: I run every story past him before I use it on the platform or in my writing. If he seems the least bit hurt, it's history. However, 99 percent of the time he loves it and adds another funny line or two of his own. Second, I make certain that for every one of those good-natured ribbings, I share two kinder comments about him.

Women are so used to "male-bashing" humor that I find the more I praise Bill in public, the more women come up to me afterward, conviction on their faces, saying, "Listening to you, I realized that I never say positive things about my husband. That is going to change as of tonight."

We know this truth from experience: "to do good and not evil" to the man we love is not only the right thing, it's the smart thing. Sooner or later, those kind words and deeds just might head back in our direction.

7
Till Death
(or High Water)
Do Us Part

. . . all the days of her life.
Proverbs 31:12b NKJV

*T*rue Love knows no age boundaries, according to Loretta from Kentucky. Her daughter came home from her first week at kindergarten and announced that she was in love with a boy in her class. Her father said, "Don't you think you're a little young?" She replied brightly, "No, Daddy. He's five and I'm five!"

Bill and I were nearly three decades older when True Love came a'calling. It was Valentine's Day, 1986, and we were exactly one month away from our wedding day. On that cold, wintry holiday evening, Bill had driven seventy miles in a blinding snowstorm to present me with my favorite flowers: red tulips. In February. No doubt about it, it was True Love.

Not to be outdone, I had spent the afternoon slicing apples into tiny slivers and rolling out a from-scratch crust to make a dessert fit for my prince: French apple pie. Classical music, candlelight on the coffee table. "Wasn't marriage going to be bliss?" I thought to myself as we cuddled on the couch and watched the falling snow.

Valentine's Day, 1995: Nine years, several pounds, and two children later. A bigger mortgage, much more laundry, two cars brimming with fast food bags and Sunday school take-home papers. No tulips. No apple pie. No snow. No doubt about it, it was . . . True Love.

Not Hollywood love. Not love at first sight. Not convenient love. Not conditional love. The Real Thing. Love based on commitment, on acceptance, on day-in, day-out, never-mind-the-seven-year-itch perseverance. It's not always exciting. In fact, it would make a dull soap opera script. Barbara Bush once said, "I married the first man I ever kissed. When I tell my children that, they just about throw up." That's True Love for you. Love for the long haul, whenever it begins.

As is the custom now, we had our wedding videotaped. It's a good thing because the entire day was one happy blur. I was so proud of us, both sentimental fools, for not crying a drop. We sang, we laughed, and the guests almost clapped when we turned to be introduced: "Ladies and gentleman, Dr. and Mrs. William Higgs!" It was an evening of transcendent joy.

But now, when I watch the videotape, I cry like a baby. "Look how young we were!" I sniff. The tears really start to roll when we begin repeating our vows. *What were we saying?* I think, shaking my head.

We were saying we would do several outrageously difficult things for the rest of our natural lives, stuff that would be hard to do for a week unless it were really True Love. Here are four of those promises many of us made.

"For Better or for Worse . . ."

This one is easy to say when we don't know how much worse it will get. Our brief, mostly-through-the-mail courtship meant we each could keep up a good "I've got it all together" front right up until we married. Imagine our surprise when we were thrown into a small car on a long honeymoon that nearly ended in divorce. (Well, not really, but for a few minutes there in Roanoke, Virginia, the future of our marriage looked dim.)

Elma from Wisconsin has one vivid memory of her wedding day in February 1958: it was cold. How cold was it? So cold that at their reception, a woman who was helping serve the food came out and announced, "The pickle juice is frozen!" Everyone had to keep their coats on to stay warm, and one man set his scarf on fire getting too close to the heater. When a marriage starts out worse, it can only get better!

If the experts are right, and romance cools 80 percent in the first two years of matrimony, how do we go the distance all the days of our lives? I say, the more surprises we can get out of the way before the wedding day, the better. One of the advantages of marrying a little later in life is it reduces some of the guess-work. In my case, I never have to worry, "Gosh, I wonder what Bill will look like without hair someday?" I already know. He never has to say to himself, "Gee, I wonder what Liz will look like someday if she lets herself go?" I'm already gone.

Melissa in South Dakota admits that she and her husband look enough alike to be related, but not *this* related. After finishing a meal in a restaurant, they were asked by their waitress how they'd like the bill divided. Melissa's husband said, "Put them both together" and paid for it by check. The waitress looked at the check and said, "Oh! You're husband and wife. I thought you were brothers." Melissa said, "We couldn't help laughing, but if it's true that the longer a couple is together, the more they look alike, we could be in trouble. After all, I don't want to lose my hair too!"

Bill and I knew that we had finally moved beyond the honeymoon stage of our relationship when one evening he suggested, "How about we tuck the kids in early and pay bills?"

Water, Water, Everywhere . . .

Dr. Joyce Brothers reminds us, "Marriage is not just spiritual communion and passionate embraces; marriage is also three meals a day, sharing the workload, and remembering to carry out the trash." Or, in our case, carrying out the water.

We can trace almost every *really* hairy moment in our relationship to an excess of water. In one house that had ground level casement windows, a hard rain guaranteed water in the basement. Not a puddle, a lake. We tried nailing the windows shut, caulking them shut, sandbagging them shut, but when the rains came, the water came in. Bill threatened to build an ark in our basement to hold not two of every species but all the soggy boxes full of books, clothing, and toys that he invariably found floating in the flood.

In that same house, the hot water heater didn't just stop working, it collapsed one day, pouring forty gallons of water all through that same wet basement. Not long after, a leaky sink put nasty water stains on the ceiling of our back bedroom. Then, when we had a second floor bath put in, the plumber punctured the hot water pipes in the wall and . . . well, you get the idea. It was always water. I started calling Bill "Noah."

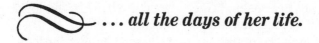 *. . . all the days of her life.*

One month before Matthew was born, I was sent home from work by my doctor. She said, "Liz, you have got to get those ankles up in the air!" Not straight up, you understand, but elevated above my hips so the swelling would go down. A necessary move, because my ankles did look ridiculous. "Squisshh! Squisshh!" they went when I walked. I couldn't wear open-toed shoes, or the water ran out.

So there I was one afternoon in my ninth month, ankles dutifully up, as I sat in an appropriately overstuffed chair and chatted on the phone with my friend Debra. In the laundry room a few feet away, I'd just put in a load of clothes. The washer was sounding unusually loud, and I knew I should put the phone down and check on it, but that would've required getting out of the chair, a seven-minute ordeal of huffing and puffing. Instead, I reached over and shut the door to the laundry room and kept right on talking. For an hour. (This is not difficult for me.)

When I finally hung up the phone, I knew something was very wrong because the washer was still running. Even on the longest cycle, it doesn't go an hour. I struggled out of the chair, made my way to the laundry room, and opened the door.

It was not a pretty sight. The washer hose was loose and spraying hot water everywhere, as it had been for an hour. The walls, the curtains, the ironing board, the piles of clean laundry, *everything* was dripping wet. But, that's not all. This laundry room had a hardwood floor, so the water had also gone through the cracks and down through the subfloor and right into my husband's basement office. That same office where he had, days earlier, gotten organized for the first time in our short married life and put up nice neat shelves with all his books and papers.

Afraid to look, but knowing I had to, I waddled to the top of the basement steps and peered down. Just as I had feared, all his books and papers were floating around about the second step.

Of course, I had to call him. "Bill!" I wailed into the telephone, summoning all my prenatal hysteria for a sympathy vote. "Bill! There's . . . there's water everywhere!"

He almost shouted into the phone. "I'll meet you at the hospital in five minutes!"

"For Richer or for Poorer . . ."

By the time our wedding day arrives, most of us have a pile of gifts that would fill two station wagons, an envelope stuffed with cash and checks from loved ones, not many bills yet, probably two incomes, and few financial worries. The grass looks greener indeed when we leap over the matrimonial fence. But eventually, things change.

Over the years, Bill and I have created budgets based on plentiful and budgets built around pitiful. The day we married, we had two incomes. Two months later, we dropped to one salary when his one-year teaching contract expired. It was not an unexpected situation, but the ensuing financial frustrations were. Add to that the stress of looking for work and our desire to start a family, and we were up to our elbows in newlywed tension.

A job was found, the money picture brightened, and we were back on an even keel for a few months. Then, I got pregnant. Hooray! Uh-oh. Now what? We saved like mad, only to watch the government take it all away at tax time.

The summer of 1987 will be remembered for three major monetary moves: I left my full time radio career, saying good-bye to 75 percent of our family income; I started my speaking career and immediately needed money for a brochure; and our first child was born.

The good news: a young mother who is home, breast-feeding her child, and handling all the household duties, does not spend much money. We were amazed at how little we missed the additional income. I continued to do a weekend radio show to keep some steady money coming in (and to have five hours to myself!). That was the best thing I could ever have done for all three of us. I got to keep my foot in the door of my old career while I established my new one, Bill got thrown into parenting every Saturday and learned How to Do Dad, and our precious baby got to have some uninterrupted time with his father. Except for not having much cash, we were very rich.

"In Sickness and in Health . . ."

Other than the usual aches and pains of moving into midlife, Bill and I have been blessed with good health and little sickness, unless you count the eighteen months of our marriage that I spent "with child."

The physical state known as pregnancy may be healthy for the baby, but it can be rough on Mom—and no picnic for Dad, either, in his role as Coach. Morning sickness, an itchy tummy, backaches, headaches, indigestion, stretch marks—the list of maladies goes on and on. With gratitude we note that it *always* ends—eventually.

My memories of being pregnant neatly divide into the three trimesters. The first trimester featured the exhaustion phase. All I wanted to do was *sleep*. So I did, anywhere I could get away with it. At my desk, on the phone, in the tub, at red lights, you name it.

During the second trimester, all I wanted to do was *eat*. As Dave Barry points out, a pregnant woman is indeed eating for two, but the other one is not Orson Welles.[1] Near the end of those middle three months were some exciting tests to assure everyone that, yes, that was a baby in there. I heard the heartbeat go "sshhwwoooop! sshhwwoooop!" Then, I felt the baby move and spent the next several weeks grabbing Bill's hand and saying, "Here! Here! Can't you feel it?"

During my visits to the doctor, I also discovered an interesting comparison game going on. I found myself feeling superior to those newly pregnant women sitting around the waiting area who looked merely tired and a bit overwhelmed. Then I'd look at the women who were further along than I was and feel humbled by their obvious seniority in these matters. Complete reverence was reserved for those women who were back in the office for their post-partum check-up, babe in arms, who clearly had made it to The Other Side.

"Till Death Do Us Part . . ."

Some people say, "As long as we both shall love," but Bill and I decided to go for a life term and stuck with the traditional, "till death do us part." The phrase "all the days of your life" shows up in Scripture two dozen times, reminding us some choices really are forever.

When we make this vow, we do so blissfully ignorant of the promise we're making and often ill-equipped to fulfill that pledge when serious illness or death comes our way.

I have a friend whose husband was diagnosed with multiple sclerosis just when their children were about to leave the nest and they were ready to be a twosome again. They are . . . but not as she had hoped.

> I'm a widow whose husband hasn't died yet. It's been a grim series of adjustments—deny, accept, accommodate—over and over again. My lover and friend are now neither. He is waiting to die, and my life is in neutral. "For better or for worse" comes to mind each time I feel I want to run away from this. Lost dreams haunt both of us, and time ticks away. We are both trying to do what is right. I find hope and solace in laughter. I try to see every beautiful thing that passes my way. Whenever my mouth upturns, I know it's good.

The Amplified version says, ". . . as long as there is life within her." For this woman, the signs of life are good, if not always joyful. By honoring her vows, even in such difficult circumstances, she earns our respect and deserves our applause.

8
Sew What?

**She seeks wool and flax, / And
willingly works with her hands.**
Proverbs 31:13 NKJV

With this verse, Lemuel and his mother have left me behind in the dust. I'm allergic to wool, and "flax" sounds like what my two kids give me when I tell them it's time for bed (flack x 2 = flax). I can't sew a straight line without raising my voice, and my attempts at dressmaking look "homemade" not "handmade." I managed a C in junior high home ec only because our teacher graded on a generous curve.

Those on the higher end of the curve are still sewing today. I am friends, it seems, with most of them, who lavish me with their handiwork at holiday time. Had I lived during biblical times, sewing would have been a necessity, not merely a pleasurable pursuit. Today, many women—by choice!—quilt, sew, crochet, macrame, knit one, pearl two, embroider, cross-stitch, smock, appliqué, and create lace *from scratch* (or whatever you make lace from).

Shirl from Kentucky remembers leaving on a long trip and taking her afghan-in-progress to keep her occupied. As they drove along, she mentioned to her husband, "The car heater seems to have something wrong with it. It's getting warmer and warmer in here." Not wanting to discourage her, he suggested, "Maybe you might like to make a smaller project." Looking down, she realized that the harder she worked, the more the afghan grew and—of course—the hotter she got!

Intent on learning the fine art of quilting, I once signed up for a six-week course with a master quilter. I made it through the first hour, during which she handed out templates and fabrics and tiny needles and a hoop and directions in such small print they gave me a headache. Finally, when we took a fifteen-minute break, I gently handed back all her materials and asked: "Can I just buy the quilts?"

I Was Needled into It

Not that I don't keep trying to teach my hands new tricks. A few years ago, I bravely attended a weekend retreat for women who are craft conscious. This was a loosely knit affair (pun intended), a gathering of women whose sole intent was to talk, eat, and quilt for two days—no classes, no breakout sessions, no speakers (although they did make me stand up and tell a funny story).

At first, I loved seeing their works-in-progress: exquisite comforters, delicate baby clothes, intricate tatting. By Saturday morning, I was beginning to feel a bit out of the loop, so a friend and I slipped away after breakfast and headed to a nearby craft supply store. I found the perfect project for my skill level: "Counted Cross-Stitch for the Inept," it was called. The finished size was 3" by 3", and it featured a single color of floss on 11-point Aida cloth. My partner assured me, "Anybody can do counted cross-stitch," so I paid for my stash and we headed back to the retreat. I practically danced through the door; finally, I would feel like "one of the girls."

I'm sure many a woman there had to stuff her face in a pillow to keep from laughing as I struggled with the oversized needle and long black strands of floss. Tentatively, I began to poke at the cloth. *Down, up. Down, up.* Look at the pattern again. *Down, up. Down, up.* Does it matter what it looks like underneath? *Down, up. Down.* Uh-oh. A knot. A knot! Now what?

Three hours of that nonsense and the whole mess went back

in the paper bag, where it has been lying dormant ever since. That was 1992. Stay tuned.

Treasured Possessions

These dear friends and others who have gifted me with their creations over the years could only guess at how their handwork has touched my life. Over a desk in our office is the cross-stitched phrase: "Working for the Lord doesn't pay much, but the retirement plan is out of this world!" Mary Jane did that in 1982. It's still there, still beautiful. On the bulletin board is a heart-stopping embroidered heart in red-on-ivory, my "corporate colors," done by Sandi, an incredible client who *paid* me too! An upstairs bedroom displays framed calligraphy done by a radio listener years ago, to commemorate the birth of Matthew in 1987: "A son is a grin with sneakers." In our bedroom sits a basket handwoven by my mother-in-law, Christmas 1988. The quilt our realtors gave us when we moved into our new/old house hangs in my son's room. The birdhouse wreath from the women of the UMC in Elizabethtown graces an upstairs window. And my feet stay warm in furry handstitched slippers from some Alaskan sisters, who retreated with me one October weekend.

And angels, lots of angels, in fabric, ceramic, corn silk, wood, stained glass, even one made from an old quilt. These gifts are so personal, so infused with love and care, that you can be sure they'll never end up in a closet, let alone a yard sale.

That's not to say there haven't been some unusual handcrafted items that have crossed my path over the last decade. One favorite comes to mind. When I helped some firemen kick off a safety campaign many years ago, they presented me with a steel hatchet, mounted on a big wooden plaque. It weighed a ton, but I felt obliged to hang it on my office wall. After all, if I'd left it tucked under my desk, I could've been arrested for concealing a deadly weapon.

Bloom Where You Are Planted

Then there was that trip to Illinois a few years ago. After speaking all day for a women's event, I was gathering up my goodies and commenting on how beautiful all the silk floral decorations had been. An enthusiastic woman stepped forward to tell me she had designed them herself. "They really are exceptional!" I assured her, which prompted her to grab a huge arrangement at the registration table and hand it to me. "Enjoy!" she said, beaming. The colors were my favorite, red and ivory, and I knew they would be just the thing for my living room. I thanked her many times as we headed for the door.

When Bill and I arrived home the next afternoon, I began walking my new silk arrangement around the house, looking for the perfect place to put it. The dining room turned out to be the best choice, but the milk glass vase was all wrong for my decor. Replacing it with a tall basket that had gone begging for attention, I tossed the milk glass vase in the kitchen wastebasket and forgot all about it.

Two days later, the phone rang. It was the generous woman from Illinois, in a major panic. "Remember the floral arrangement I gave you?" she began, almost gasping for air. "You're welcome to keep the flowers, but that vase is a valuable antique of my mother's, and she just called me and asked me if I'd seen it. Would you mind very much sending it back?"

Mind? Would I mind? Dear friends, my *mind* was blank. Where had I put that bumpy little vase? "Why, of course I'd be happy to return it, but it may take me a few days to find . . . just the right box for it," I stammered, buying time while my mind was whirling. I jotted down her address, hung up the phone, and began tearing the kitchen apart. Retracing my steps from the moment The Arrangement entered the house, I soon realized where the vase went.

I am a blessed woman. The trash bags were still by the curb, not yet picked up by the sanitation crew, so I headed out to hunt for my buried treasure. Rather than stick my hands down into that nasty collection of who-knows-what-all, I began rubbing the outside of all the Hefty bags, feeling for the familiar shape of a vase, the telltale bumps of milk glass. Bag after bag I went, rubbing and squeezing. (Months later, while collecting donations for the American Heart Association, a neighbor confessed she watched me from her window that day, squeezing my trash bags, and laughed till she cried.)

At last, I found the vase. Ripping through the plastic to pull it out, I was relieved to see that it was still in one piece and none the worse for two days in trashland. A thorough scrubbing and it was good as new . . . for an antique.

Happy Hands

The list of things I'm *not* skilled at doing with my hands is laboriously long, but I can do a few crafty things. Creating small, wooden candle boxes is one of them, especially if you like the primitive look.

For the uninitiated, this means you visit a craft store and buy pine candle boxes, already assembled. You paint them all one color with craft paint, using a large sponge brush that even a four-year-old could handle. When the paint dries, you give the wooden box to your dog to play with for an afternoon, so it gets what craft people call a "distressed" appearance. Ta-da! You've just created a Country Primitive. We gave these as Christmas gifts one year, to rave reviews. (We didn't have a pet at the time, so I "distressed" them myself. Very therapeutic.)

> *She seeks wool and flax, / And willingly works with her hands.*

Stenciling is another way I work with my hands "in delight" (NASB) and "with eager hands" (NIV). Again, it's child's play. Tape stencil on surface. Rub paint over open holes. Lift off stencil (that's the tricky part), and move to next spot. Tape stencil on surface . . . and so on. My problem is, I never do any craft half way. Once I latch on to it, I start buying things in bulk, visions of having my own booth at the Christmas Bazaar dancing in my head. Bill has caught on to me and insists on "one project at a time" purchases.

Some of us know precisely what tasks our husbands would like us to direct our busy hands toward: "Take better care of my car," wrote Gale; "finish *one* craft project," said Shirley; "fix something electrical!" was Karen's contribution; and Mary Jo knew her husband would be thrilled if she would "refinish all the painted wood in the house."

"If only I had time to pursue such things!" many of us fret. Our "want to do" list is three times longer than our "must do now" list. One woman from Michigan has chosen a full-time career as a homemaker, yet often finds it difficult to justify her choice of occupation to other women. "Everybody acts as though you're a disgrace or an alien, but I enjoy being at home, making things from scratch, sewing and doing crafts. I have time and the desire to develop my God-given talents."

To those who are so called and gifted, I say, "Brava!" I also say, "Any interest in four cases of Williamsburg blue craft paint?"

9

From the Distant Shores of the Piggly Wiggly . . .

~

She is like the merchant ships, /
She brings her food from afar.
Proverbs 31:14 NKJV

*F*ew women could draw much encouragement from being compared to a "merchant ship": bottom heavy and in need of paint! All the translations of this verse were almost identical, though the Living Bible adds some insight: "She buys imported foods, brought by ship from distant ports."

I often bring food from afar . . . literally. When I speak in Texas, I always hit the airport gift shop and buy my husband his favorite "cowboy caviar," a hot salsa stuffed with peppers, corn, jalapeños, and other veggies that make smoke come out of your ears.

Since lots of our foods today, from pineapple to coffee, arrive by boat, that should easily get us off the hook on practicing *this* verse. In fact, my understanding of "she brings her food from afar" in the modern vernacular is "she hits the drive-thru window." In my first book, a little volume of humor called, *Does Dinner in a Bucket Count?*, I concluded that it's the woman who's holding the bucket, and not what's in it, that should matter most to her family!

For good or for bad, I have perfected the art of eating while driving. I can hold a juicy burger in one hand, carefully keeping the foil around it to catch drips, while zipping through traffic. I've even been known to eat coleslaw with a "spork" at 60 mph. After all, isn't that why they call it fast food?

Kim from Kentucky confessed, "We have elderly neighbors who spend their hours looking out the windows. When I pull up at the end of the day, sometimes I hide the Wendy's bag in my purse so they won't wonder if I ever fix a decent meal for my family."

She's not the only one who turns to Wendy or the Colonel. I get help from friends—Mrs. Paul, Sara Lee, and the Jolly Green Giant—whenever possible. Karla defined the perfect wife as "a woman who is creative with leftovers." On my own job resume for "excellent wife," the notes scribbled in the margin read: "can't cook, can't sew, can dance a little."

Food That Sticks to Your Ribs (and Everything Else)

Sandy from Pennsylvania and I are kissing cousins when it comes to our kitchen abilities. She was preparing chicken croquettes—as she describes them, "the ready-made, junk food kind that probably rot your stomach, but my husband likes 'em, so who am I to argue?" She describes the story as such:

> The croquettes take forty minutes to cook, the frozen french fries he likes with them take twenty. At the end of the first twenty minutes, it was time to put the french fries in there on the other end of the same cookie sheet. Sounds simple, right? With a meal like this, you could figure on not having much mess to clean up, right?
>
> I opened the oven door, set the bag of frozen fries on the open door while I slipped on my oven mit so I could pull out the cookie sheet ... and then it dawned on me that I had just melted the entire plastic bag onto the inside of the hot oven door! My only recourse at this point, since the croquettes are half-baked (like the rest of us), is to put the salvageable fries onto the cookie sheet and shut the oven door. This bakes the plastic on there even harder. Don't ask me what I would do without my poor overworked, under-appreciated husband, who spent half of the next day with a razor blade getting the words "Ore Ida" off the glass oven door.

It warms my heart when I read mealtime horror stories from other families. Like Rita from Pennsylvania who insisted on saving all the drippings from meats thinking, "I'm going to make something out of this someday." On one occasion, after making steamed clams, she poured the copious amounts of broth into—what else—a juice container. The next morning her husband looked in the refrigerator and thought, "Oh, boy—grapefruit juice! We haven't had that for a long time," and poured himself a tall, frosty glass.

As she tells it, "When this unexpected flavor reached his taste buds, he knew it didn't taste right but figured it was because he had just brushed his teeth, so he kept right on drinking until his taste buds finally got his attention." On other occasions, Rita's ham broth was mistaken for iced tea, and family members made sandwiches using "butter" from margarine tubs that turned out to be storage containers for vanilla icing (well, it *would* look the same). Rita says, "I need a sign on my fridge that says, 'Enter At Your Own Risk!'"

Soup's Off!

Lord Byron once said, "Ever since Eve ate apples, much depends on dinner." Men do enjoy bragging about a wife who cooks well. According to some of our eight hundred women, their husbands would love it if they "would cook wonderful meals—any meals," said Marilyn; "won the Pillsbury Bake Off," wrote Patricia; "cooked more—nagged less," admitted Ila. I thought Bill might say he'd love more home-cooked meals— from someone else's kitchen.

Meal preparation is a real sore spot in many households. Who will shop for it? Who will fix it? Who will clean up the mess? These are volatile subjects in some families. More than one nasty argument has begun with the innocent question, "Honey, what's for dinner?" Among those we surveyed, cooking was handled by the woman of the house 58 percent of the time and by husbands only 6 percent. In 31 percent of marriages, women and men split the cooking duties. (I think the other 5 percent eat out!)

Mary Ann from New York offers some advice from her older and wiser perspective: "When I was married about a year, my husband suggested one day that he bake a cake for dinner. I acted very insulted and asked why he didn't like my baking. Needless to say, he didn't bake the cake and never offered to do so again through thirty-five years of marriage. I wish we could live that day over again—I would have handed him the pans and ingredients!"

Diana from Georgia remembers a hectic time in her life when she was going to college full-time and trying to be mother to her sixteen-year-old daughter and wife to her hard-working hubby. One night when she was studying for finals, her daughter announced there was nothing edible in the house. "It was getting close to 11:00 P.M., I was trying to study, my daughter was doing homework, and my husband was already asleep. I was furious. I marched up the steps, woke him, and demanded that he go to the grocery store *now*. The dear man crawled out of bed, got dressed, came downstairs, and said, 'Where is the grocery list?' I burst into tears!"

I think the whole meal situation could be more manageable

at our house if I did a better job of grocery shopping. Too often we eat out, go the bag/bucket/box route, or have pancakes— that's our "special" meal when the only things in the house are milk, flour, and eggs!—not because I don't want to cook but because the cupboard is bare. I promised you this book would have no tips, but I will share one good idea we've implemented.

I prepared a computerized list of all our favorite grocery items, by category, in the order they appear in the store. (Very organized for my personality type, I know.) By keeping one on the fridge at all times and circling things we need as we run out, it makes a trip to the grocery far more efficient. Bill really doesn't expect me to be Betty Crocker; Betty Boop with a full refrigerator is fine.

It was encouraging to read the comments of other cooking-impaired women who knew their husbands would be so proud of them if they "could plan meals ahead," wrote Wanda, or "remembered to make the coffee the night before," said Sharon, or just "filled the ice cube trays," said Barbara.

She is like the merchant ships, / She brings her food from afar.

Marilyn from Michigan admits, "One of the tasks I always disliked (and, of course, felt guilty about) was packing my husband's lunch. I was always so glad when it was done." One day he came home from work and described biting into his sandwich, only to sink his teeth into the round cardboard from the bologna package. (At least I can say I've never served cardboard—not *real* cardboard, anyway.)

Janine from California wanted her first home-cooked meal to be memorable. It was. Knowing that her new husband enjoyed Jell-O, she made a gelatin mold but added too much water, and it wasn't firming up fast enough. So she put it in the freezer. At mealtime, she took the Jell-O mold out and put it onto a plate. "It was as if the Jell-O had come to life. This large red blob started oozing off the plate on all sides and onto the table, headed in every direction. So much for my perfect dinner!"

Becky from Tennessee's four-year-old once explained to her mother just how to make Jell-O: "Take red sand, mix it with very hot water, add some ice blocks, put it in the refrigerator, and leave it until it can wiggle!"

Make Mine a Happy Meal

Getting our kids to eat what we fix for them is sometimes challenging. Rosi from Kentucky remembers when her four-year-old son wanted a piece of cake but didn't want to finish his dinner first. "Mommy," he asked, "if I don't eat my dinner, what will you do with my cake? Give it to some little boy who'll appreciate it?" That same young child was overheard telling his five-year-old brother, "Jesus might come tonight!" To which his brother replied, "I hope so. Then I won't have to eat my burrito!"

Eating out can produce some fond family memories too. Linda from Arkansas remembers a breakfast trip to a restaurant. Looking at the menu, her younger son saw "poached eggs" and asked his older, smarter brother what that was. His serious reply? "Oh, you know, those are eggs from chickens caught illegally."

Dauna from Ohio remembers the day the kids in her third-grade classroom were cleaning up at the end of the day. "Pick up the debris from your area and put it in the waste can," she told them. One little boy looked puzzled and asked, "What's debris?" "Debris is leftover junk," she replied. "Oh yeah," he said with understanding spreading across his face. "My mom fixes debris for dinner sometimes."

Living Bread

Although I spent the first two dozen years of my life in Lancaster County, Pennsylvania, I had never heard of Amish Friendship Bread. One day a friend brought me a small loaf of it and I was hooked. "Do you want some 'starter'?" she asked. Even though it sounded to me like something you put in your car, I said, "Sure!"

She showed up the next day with a bag of glop and a recipe that had obviously been photocopied dozens of times. The instructions were very clear: "*Do not* use metal spoon or bowl when mixing! *Do not* refrigerate! *Expel air* from bag occasionally." Then this ominous note: "It is *normal* for batter to thicken, bubble, and ferment." And they want me to eat this? Too late. I'd already eaten it.

"Okay, what do I do first?" I asked her.

"Nothing."

"You mean you just set it on the counter?"

"Right. And *do not* refrigerate!"

Got that. "What about tomorrow?"

"Squeeze it."

"You gotta be kidding!"

"Read the recipe. Days Two, Three, Four, and Five it just says, 'Squeeze Bag.'"

Now, this is my kind of baking. Day Six you have to open the bag and add some flour, sugar, and milk. But no fridge. Yuck. Three more days of squeezing, then the contents of the bag move to a big bowl. More flour, sugar, and milk. Then—here's where starter is born—you divide the glop evenly into four Ziploc bags and give three of them to friends.

I am doomed! I do not have three friends who cook! Bill, however, is elated at the thought of taking bags of glop to work and carries three off Monday morning with fresh photocopies of the infamous recipe. Finally, it's time to get serious about turning the glop into bread. I pour the fourth bag of glop into a bowl—*not* metal!—and stir in oil, vanilla, eggs, and baking power. That's not a typo, that's what the recipe said I needed: "1-1/2 teaspoons of Baking Power." Heaven knows, I've needed that for years.

More ingredients are added, including "1 Large Box Vanilla Pudding." One wonders how big they made boxes of pudding when this recipe was first written. At the discount shopping clubs, you can now buy one box of pudding that will feed an entire Middle School. I guess at how large they mean "Large" to be, dump the batter into two pans that have been sugared (not floured), and bake for one hour.

The problem is, you have now baked your starter and you are left with nothing to squeeze for the next ten days, until Friends One, Two, and Three all give you back a new bag of starter (actually, your own starter in another life—hard to believe the Amish would go for reincarnation like this). In theory, the Friendship Bread I'm eating today could have molecules of the original starter from, say, Noah's mother. Imagine: centuries of starter, from Joan of Arc to Joan Baez, all in my mixing bowl. Maybe this is what Mother meant when she said, "Don't touch that! You never know where it's been."

A new, more immediate concern comes into view. Let's say you have a bag of three-day-old starter, plus another one from last week, and a third bag of glop walks in the door. It could take a separate calendar just to keep track of which one to squeeze when, or who needed stirring (*do not* use metal spoon). Or what if someone accidentally made their bread on Day Nine? Would it hold their oven hostage for twenty-four hours? Or, worse, what if you don't get around to tossing the Baking Power in there until Day Twelve? Will the bowl become a small nuclear device?

With a sigh of relief, I get to the final note at the bottom of the recipe: "This bread is forgiving." (Thanks, I needed that.) "If you miss a few days, just squeeze daily until you can bake it." It sounds so heartless, until I realize that's the same method I've used to keep my family happy for the last nine years: a quick squeeze, a kiss on the cheek, an "I promise we'll have more time together soon!" and I'm off to play in other kitchens.

My Amish neighbors may be on to something. Time to bring home my flour from afar and bake some bread. First, I need a friend with starter . . .

10

Rising Is Necessary— Shining Is Optional

~

She also rises while it is yet night, /
And provides food for her household.

Proverbs 31:15 NKJV

*I*n a book called *Get It All Done and Still Be Human,* authors Tony and Robbie Fanning offered this bit of sage advice: "A stretch of uninterrupted quiet to do something on your own can be hard to find if you live with others. Overlooked solution: Get up earlier or stay up later than everyone else." Wait a minute. That solution has been around at least 2,500 years, and this verse from Proverbs proves it.

My feet have hit the floor early hundreds of mornings, but few of them were by choice. Like those nights when caffeine/adrenaline/hormones/whatever make my eyes pop open at 4:00 A.M. and refuse to close again. I toss, I turn, I engage in a round of Quilt Wars with Bill, and I give up and get up. Once awake, I get tons of work done in that quiet house, but by 11:00 A.M., I'm ready for a little nappie.

Donna from Missouri said her husband would be so proud of her if she "got up at 6:00 A.M. every morning." At our house, you would have to specify, "Kitchen Standard Time," because that's the only clock that is consistently right. The bathroom clock is fast, which means if I'm brushing my teeth and look up at the time, panic ensues. Then, I step into the hallway, which features a clock that runs slow, so I sigh with relief and take my time about putting on my makeup. Arriving downstairs, I see the inerrant kitchen clock and hysteria resumes . . . it's later than I thought! I know what you're thinking: get a watch, Liz. I have six of them, which all move at different speeds. Some aren't even in the same time zone. Maybe I should be like the woman I saw once who was wearing a watch on a choker necklace, high and tight around her neck. Then, I could walk up to people, lift my chin, and ask, "What time is it?"

Baby Time

Time goes out the window when the children arrive anyway. Our firstborn showed up seventeen months after we married . . . and two weeks late. When we pulled into the hospital parking garage, the best parking spaces by the door had big signs: "Labor and Delivery Patients Only—15 Minutes." Beneath which a wise labor and delivery nurse had written, "Push! Push!"

I had my "What to Take to the Hospital" list in hand and a whole sack of goodies, as instructed:

- A small paper bag for hyperventilating (or to blow up and smash when things got dull)

- A plastic rolling pin for backache massage (or for tossing at Bill in a heated moment)

- Sugarless lollipops (good heavens, who is counting calories at a time like that?!)

- Heavy socks in case you get cold feet (that's ridiculous; during labor, it is *much* too late to get cold feet about having a baby!)

- A sandwich or other snack for Dad (Bill ate three complete meals in front of me, while I labored and couldn't touch a bite)

- A bottle of champagne (excellent for giving self-same husband a knot on the head for falling asleep just when the contractions were picking up speed)

- A going-home outfit for the new mother (get real—whatever you wore to the hospital will still fit beautifully)

One research study I read indicated that 85 percent of fathers have a strong fear of getting queasy in the delivery room. In truth, they almost never faint or do anything else to embarrass themselves, but Bill did indeed worry about how he might react to the whole thing.

I'm just glad he was there. As labor progressed, I begged him to find some passage from the Bible to encourage me. My Hebrew scholar consulted the concordance and solemnly read aloud the following passage:

> Pains have seized me like the pains of a woman in labor.
> I am so bewildered I cannot hear, so terrified I cannot see.
> My mind reels, horror overwhelms me.
> (Isa. 21:3–4 NASB)

Thank you very much. Matthew finally made his entrance after twenty-six hours of labor. (All three nursing shifts went around and the first group came back. "She's still here!")

And what an entrance he made: eleven pounds, twelve-and-a-half ounces. Must've been that last half ounce that slowed things down. Healthy as can be and handsome to boot. I loved standing near the big glass windows of the nursery, incognito in my nightgown, as people would walk by and gawk through the glass. "Look at *that* one!" they would say. One gentleman kept looking at Matthew, then looking at me, then looking at Matthew. Finally he said, "Lady, is that your baby?" "Of course," I responded with a smile, "it's my two-year-old, in for repairs."

One of Each

Bonnie from California saw a sign in the window of her beauty shop that says: "Children by Appointment Only." What a great concept! Parents today often try to have their children spaced perfectly apart and end up perfectly spaced out. Children arrive whenever they please and please whenever they choose. We parents spend the first two years of their young lives trying to adjust to their schedules, and the next sixteen years trying to get them to adjust to ours, usually to no avail.

She also rises while it is yet night, / And provides food for her household.

Twenty months after Matthew was born, it was time for Baby Two to make the scene. A few weeks before the blessed day, my doctor ordered an ultrasound to determine the baby's size, maturity, and so forth. Bill and I hoped they could determine another important item while they were looking. We were so close to the delivery date, I thought it would be okay to find out if our new arrival would be the daughter I'd secretly wished for.

The morning of the ultrasound, I wore a pink dress and crossed my fingers. Although we would, of course, be delighted to have another wonderful son, a little sister for Matthew would have been *really* nice. I prepared myself to be jubilant, no matter what the results.

The technician was carefully scanning the screen for the pertinent information, then asked casually, "Would you like to know the sex of your baby?" "Yes!" we both chimed. "Well . . ." she said, drawing it out for dramatic effect. "You say you already have a son? Lots of little boy baby clothes? Hm-m-m-m. Looks like you'll need to do some shopping!"

Knowing ultrasounds are not always 100 percent accurate on such things, we kept our news to ourselves (but I bought *lots* of pink). When the Big Day arrived, so did Miss Lillian. A little petite thing, at ten pounds, three and three-quarter ounces. The minute Lillian let out her first wail, my very musical doctor burst into song: "Happy Birthday to You!" Not to be outdone, and under the influence of very good painkilling drugs, I sang right along with her, in harmony, "Happy Birthday, dear Lillian! Happy Birthday to You!"

Gina from Kentucky wrote to ask, "Does childbirth cause memory loss?" Yes, but I don't remember why. Apparently, Gina lives in dread of going off to work and forgetting her child. Not to worry. That's why God gave them sirens. "Wa-a-a-a-a!!"

Which gets us back to "she also rises while it is yet night." Crying babies can and do get their parents out of bed at any hour. In order to be sure we both shared this unique opportunity equally, Bill and I took turns. The first trip to the crib was his, the second was mine, the third was his and so forth. As a nursing mother, certain trips just *had* to be my responsibility, but when it came to rocking, changing, and cuddling, Daddy handled that like a pro. On the other hand, when one of our toddlers started screaming with night terrors, we both launched out of bed so fast our feet didn't touch ground until we reached the hall.

Barbara from Ohio wrote to inform me that "people say the darndest things when you are the mother of triplets!" I'll bet they do. Things like:

- "Did you *want* triplets?" (like you can place an order for multiple gestation!)

- "Are you going to have any more?" (you tell me your reproductive plans, I'll tell you mine!)

- "But you seem so calm" (am I supposed to show them my stark-raving lunatic side right away?)

Whether it's three children or five or one precious child, Kathy from Ohio summed up the motivation we all share to rise and even shine:

> I would walk through fire for my child. No matter what sacrifices, no matter what is thrown at me, my child comes first. She is worth every extra pregnancy pound, every hour of labor, every night I'm tired and just want to sleep, every dirty diaper, every throw-up, every child care dollar. I wouldn't trade her away for all the gold in the world. I bet you'd agree.

Yes, Kathy, I would.

What Comes after Breakfast?

The only directive we're given in this verse is, basically, to get up early and make them breakfast. No problem, I'm a good mother; I make breakfast every morning. Pop Tarts. Even if it doesn't specifically mention it in Scripture, we also need to be sure they scrub their hands and faces. Although, as humorist Fran Lebowitz noted, "Even when freshly washed, children tend to be sticky."

Terry from Pennsylvania wrote, "I always like reading about other moms. It validates that I'm not crazy . . . it's my kids!" Fran said, "Give moms like me the okay to fall somewhere between June Cleaver and Roseanne." Now, that's a wide path. I would say almost all of us fall in the middle, most of the time. Not to say that there haven't been a few frightfully awful days, when I might scream, hiss, bellow, eat my children's Easter candy, or exhibit all manner of beastly behavior.

Leslie from Kentucky may become concerned when she reads this book, since she wanted some "insight on what it would be like to be married, work, and have children . . . I don't know if I want to attempt this!" Oh, by all means, *attempt*. Just be ready to forgive yourself, hug your kids, ask their forgiveness, and keep on going. Dottie is hoping I will "affirm that there is still *hope* for families in this troubled world!" Hope? Absolutely. An easy time of it? Not always.

Betty from Iowa remembers when she was working nights with a new baby, four older children, and *no* washing machine(!). Keeping baby's clothes clean was a problem. She said, "Many times when I was working nights at the hospital, I brought what looked like a bag of crafts but was really baby wash, because we had a laundry there. I felt guilty many times." We mothers gotta do what we gotta do.

The One That Got Away

Sometimes we get so busy, so tired, or so distracted that things just happen. Thank goodness most of the time they have a happy ending. Becky from Indiana confessed to one incident when she and her husband took separate cars to Grandma's house for dinner. Their three-year-old daughter fell asleep, so her father carried her out to the car and moments later both parents drove off for home.

Becky arrived first and went straight to bed, figuring her

husband would be along shortly with their daughter and tuck her in. Meanwhile, he pulled in the drive and went right to bed, too, confident that since he had put the little girl in his wife's car, she had carried her up to bed. At 2:00 A.M., the doorbell rang, and a tearful three-year-old was begging to get in! "I tried a little harder after that," Becky admitted.

Mickey from Kansas had a close call on a shopping expedition with her eighteen-month-old twin girls. She had stopped at a parking lot plant sale and was pulling along the girls in one cart and the plants in another. All was going well, the twins were entertaining each other, and she had found four or five healthy houseplants and paid for them.

> I was on my way back through all the plants when I saw a nice floor plant I'd overlooked before. I stopped both carts to turn around and look at this wonderful plant, and when I turned back, my babies were heading into the parking lot loaded with cars, and my cartful of plants was rolling that way too! Of course, I went running to rescue my girls first. [Good mother.] They were having the time of their lives *until* they rammed into the front fender of a brand-new pickup truck. The poor owner hadn't even had time to get his license plate yet!
>
> The girls weren't hurt but were scared and crying. The man in the truck was nice also and handled everything with our insurance agent (who called to verify that, indeed, two toddlers really did damage this man's truck!). By the way, the plant cart struck a parked car. Thank heavens for insurance!

"The One Thing I Wish I'd Done Differently As a Mother Is . . ."

This question about mothering produced some very wise, very poignant answers from women with grown children who had done the rise and shine routine umpteen times. "I wish I'd hugged more and yelled less," said Debra from Alaska. "Not been so strict," shared Joan from Arkansas. "Spent more time with them in their beginning years," wrote Nancy from Florida.

Many responses fell into the more category: more . . . fun, hugs, time, reading, playing, listening, accessibility, kisses, positive reinforcement, consistent discipline, and from Joanne from Montana, "Said 'I love you' more often."

Others, if they could do it all over again, would have done less: less . . . dusting, work, worry, and less emphasis on a perfectly clean house.

If Patricia had a second chance, she'd "have more kids!" Sandi would have "taken more time to enjoy each stage of development." The wisdom of experience shines through Judy's words: "Learn to realize 'teenagers' are a concept that gets better only with time."

When we paint a picture of motherhood that is all rosy, all joyful, we are doing younger women a disfavor. It is not always fun, and it is almost never easy. Shirley Rogers Radl, author of the controversial book *Mother's Day Is Over,* found that facing the realities of motherhood and the less-than-thrilling aspects of the job was an important turning point in her life. She wrote that it "was a new beginning for me—the beginning of self-acceptance, growth, and the rebuilding of my rapidly vanishing self-esteem. It was also a beginning for reaching out and grabbing those joyous times and cherishing them."[1]

Some of us are working without a road map, without family role models to help us find our way. Donna insisted, "I am carving out my own path," and Janet agreed that she and her partner are "making it up as we go!" And Martha cautioned me, "Don't forget single mothers. We are often so overwhelmed with survival that humor eludes us."

Even in two-parent homes, humor can remain hidden. Mary Jane wishes she'd "had more fun with them. Not been as serious." Indeed, Sandy described the perfect parent as "one who is able to smile and relax when the dishes are piled sky high and the weeds in the front yard are up to your waist!" For those of us who feel we don't know enough, or don't do enough, to be an expert parent, pediatrician T. Berry Brazelton says, "A child needs a flexible, humorous parent more than a professional 'child development expert' parent."[2]

Oh, that we could all rise *and* shine and come to the same conclusion someday that Barbara from Utah has reached: "I have no regrets. I did my best."

11

How She Did It All

~

. . . and portions to her maidens.

Proverbs 31:15b NASB

Just when we grind our teeth over the poor Proverbs 31 woman who not only has to get up early to feed her family, but must give "portions to her maidens" as well, a little knowledge of Hebrew comes to our rescue: the word *portion* doesn't mean a serving of food, it means "assignments, duties, tasks." In other words, she got up early to *give orders!* Now, that sounds more like it. As The Living Bible puts it, she "plans the day's work for her servant girls." I take this as a biblical directive to hire help! If we're going to "rise while it is yet night," we intend to take a lot of people with us.

Of course, we already have lots more help around the house than our proverbial sister did. Dishwashers, microwave ovens, vacuum cleaners, washing machines—these mechanical marvels have certainly made life easier for us. Or have they? Less time needed for housework should, in theory, mean more time for family fun and leisurely pursuits. A recent advertisement for Whirlpool Home Appliances suggests otherwise: "If only you could duplicate yourself. Imagine how much you'd get done." Even with appliances galore, we still can't seem to plow through all our "home work." Dottie declared, "My husband and I have figured out a really good system about the housework: neither one of us does it."

Hans Hoffman said, "The ability to simplify means to eliminate the unnecessary so that the necessary may speak." Simplification at the Higgs household has meant learning to clearly say no! I can announce with some measure of pride that I have mastered this principle in at least one area: I say no to housecleaning. There are whole businesses built around my willingness to turn this task over to the professionals.

People say, "Oh, you're so lucky you can afford help." Who says we can afford it? Bill and I have agreed that even if we get down to food stamps, an occasional visit from a housekeeper is a good investment in our sanity. For those of us who truly can't afford such help right now, keep in mind the good advice I found on a notepad: "Time management begins with a very large wastebasket."

Washday Blues

Even those of us who use the pros still end up doing our own laundry. There's something about having an outsider flinging around our underwear that just doesn't sit well with me. In order to tackle this thankless task, we observe the following Three Higgs Rules of Laundry:

1. There will always be dirty laundry.

This is very difficult for a "finish-the-job" kind of woman like me to accept. I'm not happy until every piece of clothing is washed, folded, and put away. I've tried lining up my family, collecting everything they're wearing, and stuffing it in the washer, just to have it all done (they are becoming less tolerant of this method). But even then, within minutes another small pile begins to gather in the hamper.

2. If it's clean, it isn't laundry.

With two kids and a husband who all appear to wear six outfits a day, laundry can begin to take over the house. Piles here and piles there, some clean, some dirty, many of uncertain status. Often the scenario goes like this: on my way out the door to a speech, I toss a load of clothes in the washer, push start, and leave. Hours later, my baby-sitter, wanting to be helpful, gathers up a load of wash, opens the washer lid, and . . . uh-oh, clothes. Cold, wet, flat against the sides. "Wonder how long this has been in here?" she thinks. "Better run it through again." In goes the detergent, softener, and water. She pushes start, forgets all about it, and leaves.

That night Bill thinks, "I'll bless Liz and do a load of laundry." So, he collects a pile and flips open the lid . . . yikes! Stuff in there. Cold, wet, flat against the sides. "No telling how long this has been sitting," he thinks. "Better wash it again." More water, more softener, more detergent. Luckily, Bill lives at our house, so he's there when the wash cycle ends and moves everything to the dryer. Whew . . . the clothes are spared!

Except Bill has not had "Folding 101" yet, so when the dryer stops, he stuffs all those nice clean, warm clothes down into a laundry basket and leaves the basket by the machine. When I walk in the door and see that jumble of wrinkled clothes, I sigh, "Better get started on some of this laundry." Into the washer it all goes.

There are outfits that have never escaped. Bill will look at them, finally worn to a frazzle and stuffed in the wastebasket, and say, "I never even saw you in that!"

3. When in doubt, sniff.

This seems the obvious solution. If it smells like Tide, put it on.

Who's in the Kitchen?

We often assume that the female of the species is more concerned with keeping things neat and clean than her male counterpart, but some of our men like it tidy too. "My husband would be so proud of me if I . . . cleaned house every day," said Nancy, or "picked up every object on a horizontal surface," wrote Sandy, or "de-junked the closets, attic, and drawers," said Sue Anne. Then there's Laura who thinks her husband would be thrilled if she "cleaned the litter box." For the cat, I assume.

I was plain curious: who is doing the work around our houses, anyway? Eight hundred women gave me a state of the union on this subject:

- Laundry was more of a she thing than a he thing, falling into our laps 56 percent of the time, and theirs just 3 percent. We share the job 30 percent of the time.

- Dusting and other cleaning sorts of activities fall on our shoulders 39 percent of the time, on his just 4 percent of the time, and are equally shared 24 percent. More than 17 percent of us portion out cleaning duties to hired help. Good news: our kids are also helpful with dusting, at 8 percent.

What did men help with most? Changing the light bulbs. And what did they help with least, of the dozen activities I listed? Cleaning the lint trap in the dryer. (As one wife said, "First he would have to know that such a thing existed!") I was surprised that, despite rumors to the contrary, men do occasionally change the toilet tissue rolls when they are empty—sometimes without even being told to do so.

At our house, I'm the bathroom tissue changer. Had I not portioned this task to myself, in a few months small cardboard tubes with three sheets of tissue still attached would be lurking in every corner of the bathroom, on shelves, and on the back of the toilet. It's simply too important to leave to chance. For the record, 68 percent of us like it to unwind *over,* and 32 percent like it to dispense from *under* the roll. It's not simply an aesthetic decision, since research has shown that the *overs,* on the average, earn $20,000 more each year than the *unders.* It's enough to make you toss down this book and flip over those rolls *right now.*

Training Techniques

The fact is, more men would be willing to help us if they just knew where to begin. They need to be told that there is not a chromosome for domestic skills and that *we* had to learn this stuff, which means they can too! And they need lots of applause. Let's not get huffy or resentful—just start clapping. It also helps to show them exactly how we'd like tasks to be done, describing everything in detail and giving hands-on instruction when needed. Finally, we need to make it worth their while.

I am living with a success story. Bill washes 99 percent of the dishes in our house, virtually every dish! How did I manage this? I am allergic to Joy—not the experience, the dishwashing liquid. (I'm probably fine with Ivory, but I buy Joy.) Plus, Bill does 80 percent of the cooking. This is a survival move, but he also enjoys it. These days, I bring *him* cookbooks from different regions of the country, which he reads like novels then selects a recipe to try for dinner that night. Amazing.

～ *... and portions to her maidens.*

Teaching him how to clean the house was not as easy. There are lots of gadgets, sprays, rags, and mops to confuse things. Vacuuming seemed the most "macho" activity of the bunch, so I suggested he give it a try. His blank stare told me I needed to offer more instruction. A good trainer always takes a familiar idiom and grafts it onto the new concept, so that's exactly what

I did—literally. I took an old lawn mower handle, tied it onto the vacuum cleaner, pointed to the carpet, and said, "Mow!" Things were going great until he brought in the Weed Eater.

We all have our own areas of domesticity where we'd like to take advantage of our man's talents. Maryann would love her man to "run the vacuum, wash dishes, do laundry, and send flowers in the same day." Jacki agrees that an ideal husband "helps out without being asked and surprises you by cooking supper (or calling for pizza is fine too!)." For Susan, if he just wouldn't "splash water all over the mirror just after you clean it," she would be happy.

Shelly from Kansas has a helpful hubby, who washes most of their laundry and shares childcare responsibilities. "I'm so fortunate to have a helpmate like him," she wrote. "My friends often ask how I 'changed' him. I didn't change him. He was always willing to help, but he didn't know how. He learned how to do things by watching me and asking questions. I also learned if I wanted his help, I had to be less of a perfectionist! (If the dishes are put away, what does it matter that the measuring cup is on the shelf with the drinking glasses?)"

Our children are woefully underutilized in the home care department. Less than 2 percent help with cooking, about 3 percent help with laundry—this, when easily half the dirty clothes are theirs! Their fault? I doubt it. The truth is, most of us stay up till all hours, washing and folding clothes, feeling every bit the martyr, when our kids could easily be given this responsibility. My own mother never showed me how to use the washer and dryer until I went to college. I don't intend to make the same mistake, although I suppose age five is a tad young for ironing. Drat.

Linda from Pennsylvania received a needlepoint plaque from her daughter that reads, "Dust is a protective covering for furniture." Linda's response was: "Hallelujah! I generally clean only when company is expected and no one seems to mind." Her motto is, "Clean enough to be healthy and dirty enough to be happy."

Anyway, as Barbara Billingsley from *Leave It to Beaver* fame pointed out, "Even June Cleaver didn't keep her house in perfect order—the prop man did it."

12

Across the Fruited Plain

She considers a field and buys it; /
From her profits she plants a vineyard.

Proverbs 31:16 NKJV

*L*ike so many successful women today, some of our biblical role models were real estate profession- als. Women have always had a knack for buying and developing property. The text doesn't suggest that she bought and sold fields continually, but she did buy this particular one.

The Amplified translation sheds a revealing light on exactly what it meant for her to consider buying that field: "... [expand- ing prudently and not courting neglect of her present duties by assuming other duties]."

"Courting neglect?" Well, if that isn't an accurate description of me! Whenever I take on a new challenge, Bill says, "That's fine, but what activity are you going to drop in order to make this one happen?" "Drop?" I ask, with that hand-in-the-cookie-jar look on my face. "Gosh, I wasn't going to drop anything. I figured I'd just squeeze it in during the commercials."

Playing "Beat the Clock"

The time management books I've seen (and believe me, *this* isn't one of them!) all encourage us to maximize every single waking moment: exercises to do at our desk, Scripture verses to memorize at red lights, language tapes to listen to while we jog, thank-you postcards to carry in our purse for a spare second while standing in line at the bank. Sure, we can accomplish more, but the real question is, "Why?" Is all the energy output worth the information input? No wonder, when asked what we wanted less of and more of in our life, we so often paired them together like this:

We Want More . . .	And Less . . .
Sleep!	Rush, Rush, Rush!
Time off	Deadlines
Energy	Commitments
T•I•M•E	Aggravation
Time for self	Responsibility
Relaxation	60-hour work weeks
Free time	Pressure to do more

The one thing we want *more* of is the one variable we can't change: *time*. More than four hundred of us mentioned it specifically on the surveys. Yet, whether we look back to biblical times, or to the turn of any century, there have always been the same number of seconds in a minute, minutes in an hour, and hours in a day—even if we called them something else.

As the old chestnut goes, "Time flies whether you are having fun or not!" Maybe when we say we need more time, which we can't control, we really mean we need fewer items on our to do list, which we can control. Dolores from New York longed for "more priority-setting ability" and "less hesitance." No doubt about it, *no* isn't hard to pronounce, but it's very hard to say.

We know instinctively that the commitments we have taken on are wearing us out. And we want to change. Bev's words leaped off the page of her survey: "Help me out of being over-committed!" Carolyn said, "Tell me how to manage time—or how I can laugh about not having enough of it!" Kim hoped this book would "provide insight on changing (that is, lowering) your standards. How to say *no* and mean it."

That's a two-part request. First, I don't think *any* woman should really lower her standards. Rather, we should elevate those that matter the *most* and lighten up on the others. For example, as the deadline for this book approached, more and more time was spent at the computer and less and less time was spent with a feather duster in my hand. That was as it should be. The book was more important; the dusting could wait. To my knowledge, the Dust Police are not planning a visit to my house anytime soon.

One could say, "Well, if you wrote for two hours every day for a year, you could still keep the house clean *and* finish the book, and that would be more disciplined." If that's your work style, fine, but it definitely is not mine. I work in Passion Mode. When I get excited and enthusiastic about something, look out. I live, breathe, eat, and drink that subject until it has run its course, then I take a short siesta before diving into the next project.

What this means is that I must plan ahead for when passion strikes (most married women with young children already know how to do this!). In a workload sense, it means blocking out two or three months for writing (or working on whatever special project I might be involved with) during which some extra help, paid or otherwise, will be needed around the house.

By blocking out, by no means am I suggesting we exclude our loved ones. I mean, set aside other outside commitments and tackle one major project at a time. I find that the more consuming that project is, the more I cherish the routine of family life to keep me balanced and to keep my sense of humor intact. Susan from New Hampshire recalls, "One evening, while we were eating dinner, the doorbell rang. My husband left the table to answer it, and of course it was a salesman. When he came back to the table, our four-year-old daughter said, 'Who was it, Daddy?' He replied, 'A stranger.' She quickly asked, 'Did he offer you candy?'"

In the Long Run . . .

In his book, *Bonkers*, Dr. Kevin Leman noted, "Getting your priorities straight and sticking to them is one of the most difficult tasks in life."[1] What makes it easier for me is consciously listening to God's voice, my husband's voice, and my own voice as they all resonate in my heart. This requires ignoring the voices of media and peer pressure and filtering out the *you shoulds* from well-meaning but ill-informed sources.

Some questions worth asking ourselves might be:

- Will this activity matter one week from today? One month? One year?

- Is there someone who does it better than I do, to whom I might delegate this activity?

- Does it satisfy a heart need for me or someone I love very much?

- What are the ramifications if I *don't* do it?

- What are the outcomes if I *do* do it?

This exercise might be a little much for considering whether you should take out the trash. The answer there is yes! But for any activity that will require even a modest drain on our time/money/energy resources, it could provide the pause we need to reconsider and say, "No, thanks."

My daughter, Lillian, who turned five while I was functioning in Passion Mode for this book, declared, "The next time they ask you to write a book, just tell them, 'No way—I have to tuck my children into bed!'" I laughed, but I listened too. At night when the words flowed most easily, Bill would often kiss them goodnight with a promise that "Mama will see you in the morning." After Lillian's comment, I knew that Passion Mode needed to be parked for a moment while I went upstairs to hug my children and hear their prayers.

After all, look at the five questions above in light of that nightly tuck-in:

- *Yes,* those precious times will matter in years to come, to both of us.

- *No,* there is no one else who can do "Mama" better.

- *Yes,* it satisfies a heart need for me *and* for my loved ones.

- Ramifications if I don't? Disappointment for them. Guilt for me.

- Outcomes if I do? They sleep better, and I work better, knowing I took time to do something that *really* mattered.

(Uh-oh, does this count as a tip or—heavens—a list?!) Just file it under personal experience and my desire to develop good discernment in such matters.

Next to *Time,* We'd Love to Have More . . .

Money, of course, was our second choice after time, but it was a distant second. Elaine St. James, in her book *Simplify Your Life,* observed, "The secret to happiness is not in getting more but in wanting less."[2] Plenty of us feel like we have traded time for money and are now considering the impact it has had on us and our families and the fruit of our efforts to make money and mother as well.

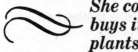 *She considers a field and buys it; / From her profits she plants a vineyard.*

According to our surveys, those of us with kids at home are averaging 42.3 hours a week at work. Throw in commuting time, plus any work that's dragged home with us, and that makes for one full week for a working mom. Although we hear plenty about mothers working half-time, part-time, or flex-time, the surveys showed that only 14 percent of working moms put in fewer than thirty hours a week, averaging nineteen hours a week at work. Part-time work often seems like the perfect solution, but Karen Hull, author of *The Mommy Book,* warns that among her friends who tried it, "working at a part-time job was like buying a five-pound turkey. By the time they got rid of the skin and bones—i.e. the hidden expense—there was very little meat left."[3]

At the other end of the scale were the nearly 18 percent of us who work more than 50 hours a week, with some exhausted mothers logging 60, 70, even 80 hours a week at work. Whew!

When asked, "What level of guilt, if any, do you feel about not being with your children full time?" 32 percent of working mothers circled eight, nine, ten, or Guilt to the Max. These women often did not feel comfortable with their childcare arrangements or with their long hours or both. In most cases, they had younger children, when the internal and external pressures to be home are strongest.

Diane notes her guilt "probably is due to outside comments." Melanie feels Guilt to the Max about putting her three children in a childcare center, even though the center is at her work site. She worries that "they spend more waking hours with strangers than at home." Pamela feels a big dose of guilt because "my mother was a full-time mom."

A Hoosier mom poignantly voiced the dilemma that many of us face: "Am I sacrificing important time with my child to provide less important tangible benefits? Are my priorities skewed? Am I being selfish?" This is a woman who loves her work, has her two-year-old son safely cared for by his grandmother, and is frankly not certain she is ready for full-time motherhood. "I'm not sure I could be as excited about mothering if that's all I did twenty-four hours a day."

Even with the best situation for our families, we experience guilt. Donna from Nevada, also with young children, also with a husband to care for them, still circled a nine on her guilt meter, saying, "I should be home, providing them a good environment." Joan admits, "It's hard when they cry when I leave in the morning." She puts her guilt at a seven, even though her kids are cared for by a competent nanny. Lissa, working mother of four, is grateful her children are in the care of their grandparents, but still circled a ten "because I remember the things I missed out on growing up when my mother worked full-time."

Mothers of older kids aren't exempt from guilt, either. Mickey is "afraid I'm missing something" when she is apart from her pre-teenagers and also worries "what others think."

All this to say: If you are struggling with these issues, you are not alone. We are all trying to find our way through the maze and onto the best path—which is not, perhaps, the same path for each of us.

On the Other Hand

Bill and I often send each other greeting cards, not just for the usual occasions, but sometimes just because. He covers them with little personal notes, artistic touches, and inside jokes, so I can't bear to toss them out. One card is dated September 1990—Matthew was three, Lillian was eighteen months old, and my speaking career had suddenly taken off. I was trying hard to gear down my business (funny—still my number one problem today), and Bill's encouraging card included this note: "It's been a long, hard day, and for that matter a long, hard week (for *that* matter, a long, hard year!!). I love you, Liz, and want to help you find a lifestyle that is fulfilling to you and yet practical for all of us. Let me love you through this tough time." He did, and he does.

As a couple, Bill and I continue to discuss, adjust, negotiate, and hammer out a lifestyle that honors God, his Word, and our own God-given abilities and desires. By staying in tune and in touch with each other, we can keep the guilt meter on low and the fruit meter on high!

Many women surveyed have found out how to do the same. Michele from Indiana circled three on the guilt meter, and wrote, "A working woman is who I am—it's the only kind of mother I know how to be." Becky is able to feel almost guilt-free because of two important considerations: "If I'm not home with the children, my husband is," and "the company I work for allows my family to come first—there are not many companies that do." Not yet, but it's coming.

The other mothers who registered nearly guilt-free are those who have chosen a work schedule that most matches their children's lives (teacher), or who have their own business (selling Mary Kay Cosmetics, Tupperware, or Longaberger Baskets) with flexible hours.

Some of us have found job situations that balance our financial requirements and mothering needs very well. Isabel from New York, whose children are both teenagers, works 20-30 hours a week so she is "there when they are, and when I'm not there, they are learning to be independent and self-reliant." Other women entrust their husbands with childcare duties, like Carol, mother to three youngsters under age five, who insists that "I'd go nutty at home. I like being a working woman . . . my husband does a super job" at home.

Alice, mother of a four-year-old, feels nearly guilt-free because "I give to him completely and easily when we are together because I'm a happy person and love my job." Many mothers echoed that experience of being really focused on their children when they are with them. And other moms wanted their children to have a wider view of life than their own living room. Susan said, "There's a lot more to this world than I alone can give them. I enjoy sharing their daily experiences and talking to them at the end of the day."

Getting Rid of the Guilt

The phrase that kept popping up under the "why I feel guilty" section was I'm too tired to ". . . cook, play, help with homework, taxi to activities, and so on." No wonder we are tired! No generation has tried to accomplish more, been offered as many choices, or faced more negative influences.

And everywhere we turn, we find someone who has The Solution. Or they hold up warning signs that do not fit our situation. Like the sign I saw in a ladies rest room in Winner, South Dakota. On the wall next to the mirror was one of those cloth towel dispensers, where the towel comes down in a loop. Above the towel dispenser was a sign that read: "Warning! Do not attempt to swing from towel."

Wait a minute . . . have you ever stepped into a rest room and found a woman swinging from the towel? The thought had never occurred to me. Now I'm looking at it. How would you do it? Put your arm in the loop? Your leg? One thing is certain: If you ever walk into a rest room now and find a towel draped all over the floor, you've been warned!

Guilt can be a warning sign, too, but it can also simply be an indicator of the need to stop and evaluate. My own approach to guilt is to change the situation or change my attitude but never sit there soaking in guilt stew!

Instead, I pray. And listen. I look at *all* the possible options before me. I put my imagination to work and come up with every method of balancing work and home life conceivable, no matter how wild or impractical they may seem on paper. Then I discuss them with my loved ones and see which ideas should be tossed, and which ones are worth serious consideration.

At some point, we may choose to bring in a professional—a counselor, a career consultant, an accountant, a financial adviser—to sort through the specifics. Especially for those of us who may be working outside of the home for only one reason— money—it would be wise to have a tax expert calculate the differences in taxes we would pay with one income versus two. Then we need to figure out exactly what working costs us in childcare, clothing, lunches, commuting expenses, and so forth. The numbers may point to a definite need to work, and that's fine. At least we'll know, and we can begin to let go of the guilt.

For a woman who has a low salary and high expenses associated with her job, it may make more sense to stay home and invest her efforts there, which might significantly lower guilt and raise joy. Until we "crunch the numbers," it's hard to say with authority "I work because we need the money."

The key is to avoid the "good mothers stay home/bad mothers go to work" message, in favor of: "A good mother does what is best for *all* the members of the family, including herself." Melodie Davis, author of *Working, Mothering and Other "Minor" Dilemmas,* thinks "it would be helpful not to think in terms of whether a working mom is 'bad' or 'good' for children. Being a good mom or a bad mom is related to how a woman feels about herself and her children."[4]

Most of us want it to be simpler than that. Those on the conservative end of things insist, "Real mothers stay home because it is our job to care for our children!" Those with a more liberal agenda might say, "Real mothers work, and it's the government's responsibility to provide childcare!" For the vast majority of us who are somewhere in the middle—grateful to be moms, grateful to be working, but not so sure how to pull it all off—it's very confusing.

Elizabeth Cody Newenhuyse, in her book *The Woman with Two Heads,* celebrates the complex nature of life as a devoted mother *and* a devoted career woman. After all, "God created complexity. No one is all one thing. The discovery of complexity, of the pain that comes with many good gifts, can free us from corrosive guilt, worry, frustration, from thinking we should manage our lives better. It's okay not to have all the answers."[5]

Good, because I don't have all the answers. I'm not even sure I'm asking the right questions when I consider the fields before me. I simply focus on serving God, loving people, and doing my best to make a difference in my own spheres of influence. It's not necessary to do more. And it's not satisfying to do less.

13
Personal Best

**She girds herself with strength, /
And strengthens her arms.**

Proverbs 31:17 NKJV

Say it isn't so . . . not aerobics and strength training in the Bible! Relax. King Lemuel's mother was not hoping to get Jane Fonda for a daughter-in-law. She wanted a bride who was "fit for a king," namely, her son. This kind of fitness comes from hard work, not from working out. An excellent woman is ready for action rather than for a life of leisure. The Living Bible says she is "energetic, a hard worker"; and, according to the New International Version, she "sets about her work vigorously." Like Shelly from Kansas described the ideal wife, she's "the 'support beam' in a home. She's the one who sets the tone for rest of the family."

The Amplified version once again gives us the whole picture, defining this strength as "spiritual, mental, and physical fitness for her God-given task." We all know, at least theoretically, how to develop physical fitness: eat healthful foods and exercise our muscles.

I love the classified ad I saw in (of all places) a decorating magazine. It listed an 800 number to call and learn about the "biggest breakthrough in the diet industry in twenty-five years!

Diet one day; eat the next twenty-four hours!" Gee, that's the way I've always done it, haven't you? Besides, as one of my favorite magnets says, "God must have loved calories—He made so many of them."

For mental fitness, we need to feed our minds positive, accurate information and put that knowledge into practice. Eleanor Doan said, "The mind is as strong as its weakest think." We never outgrow the need to expand and educate our minds. With college courses, continuing education programs, and whole libraries full of knowledge waiting for us out there, we are surrounded with food for the intellect. As Beverly Sills said, "There is a growing strength in women but it's in the forehead, not the forearm."[1]

But what about spiritual fitness? The best diet is "the pure milk of the word," (1 Peter 2:2 NKJV), "solid food . . . for the mature" (Heb. 5:14 NIV), the "fruit of the Spirit" (Gal. 5:22 NKJV), and "the bread of life" (John 6:48 NKJV). Having feasted on such fine spiritual food, we are ready to exercise "obedience" (Heb. 5:8 NKJV) and be "clothed with humility" (1 Peter 5:5 NKJV). Even One-a-Day vitamins can't produce that kind of strength in your life!

Endurance Training

I first met Dauna from Ohio through her survey, then from some of her writings, and finally in person at one of my presentations. This woman is the embodiment of how to develop spiritual and mental fitness, a mother who watched her thirteen-year-old daughter deal with the reality of her five-year-old sister's bout with cancer and who grew stronger because of it:

I tried to protect my older daughter from it all and never had her at the hospital with us when her younger sister was so very, very sick from chemotherapy. So all the older one saw was the attention showered on her sister, including hundreds of gifts and cards from friends. I'm certain she was jealous of all of it. Then, during the last round of chemotherapy, she was at the hospital working as a volunteer. It was the first time she saw how grim her little sister's hospital stays really were. It was as though a light bulb went on in her head. I believe sometimes we do a disservice to our children by protecting them from the harsh realities a little too much.

She's right: strength comes from handling adversity, not avoiding it. The strongest women I know got that way by going through, rather than around, life's mine fields. It's a workout, all right, but the spiritual muscles it produces are worth it. As Louisa May Alcott said, "I am not afraid of storms, for I am learning how to sail my ship."

She girds herself with strength, / And strengthens her arms.

Nearly half of the speaking I do is for healthcare audiences, who sail their ships through rough waters every day they show up for work. In their ongoing struggles to keep us all healthy, they are discovering that more than just the physical self is involved. Increasingly, they're seeing that mental and spiritual wellness contribute to a patient's recovery as well. In his book, *Head First: The Biology of Hope,* Norman Cousins outlined some of the positive emotions that are needed to promote healing: love, hope, faith, the will to live, festivity, purpose, and determination.[2] Sounds like the fruit of the Spirit to me.

Seeking Strengths, Finding Weaknesses

The list Cousins proposed includes the very qualities most of us want in our lives. As a means of determining our strengths and weaknesses, I asked women, "What is the one character trait you'd really like to change about yourself?" Some of the things we wrote down included:

"Have more fun"
"Less grumble, grumble, grumble"
"Listen more"
"Less quick to judge"
"More trusting that everything will work out"
"Less serious about everything"

"More passionate"

"Less procrastination, but not right now" [very funny]

Many expressed a need for increased confidence, to be "more self-assured," as Carol from Maryland put it, or as Patty wrote, to have less "self-doubt . . . right?"

Four responses seemed to surface again and again, in no particular order:

- Impatience

- Poor self-esteem

- Procrastination

- Perfectionism (what Barbara from Ohio called "nit-picki-ness")

The way I see it, all four stem from the same root problem, aptly expressed by Jan from Washington: "too high expectations of others and myself."

Expecting Too Much from Ourselves and Others—maybe we should label it the "ETMOO Syndrome!" It's safe to say that the majority of us suffer from it. Because we want things done *perfectly*, we *procrastinate* rather than do something wrong. Our realization that we are not perfect leads to *poor self-esteem*. Then, because we want others to be perfect, too, we are *impatient* with their imperfection. It's a vicious cycle, this ETMOO.

The only antidotes I can offer for this malady are grace, love, and laughter. Grace, to assure us we are forgiven for our imperfections. Love, to remind us that we are indeed valuable "as is." And laughter, to help us relax and find the humor in our less-than-perfect condition.

What Will They Think of Next?

For those of us who long to do a better job of, say, staying in touch with loved ones, there's a new software program billed as a "relationship management program designed to help you stay up to date in nine areas of your personal and business relationships." (FYI: The *perfectionists* will love this; those of us with *poor self-esteem* won't think we deserve it; the *impatient* among us may think relationships aren't worth managing; and the *procrastinators* will think it's a great idea, but will never get around to ordering it!)

Here's how it works. After we program in the necessary date information for the presumably dozens, even hundreds, of people in our lives, the computer program prompts us to review data on a person when, say, their birthday is coming up. Then, a handy database gift catalog "allows you to fax, mail, or call toll-free to order products ranging from flowers to tropical cruises with just a click of a button." Amazing. (Should my birthday produce a prompt on your screen, please click "tropical cruise.")

In theory, it's a great idea. How many times have we forgotten the birthdays of coworkers, friends, even loved ones because we neglected to check our calendars? Still, it's too calculated for me, too much hardware (the computer) and not enough software (the heart). I would hate to think that I received a birthday card generated by a PC and signed by an ink jet.

My father has a method that produces the same results—remembering important days in the lives of those he cares about—but with a much more human approach. The first of each year, he takes his long birthday list—there are more than thirty of us in his immediate family, not including great-grandkids!—and heads for the card shop. He carefully chooses a greeting card for each person, one that says exactly what he would like it to say, brings the cards home, puts on stamps, addresses them, and files them into a desk calendar by the date they should be mailed. Voila! Now that's "relationship management." Although I have yet to get a tropical cruise, a birthday card on time is a real treat.

Encouraging One Another—Even Yourself!

There's another important relationship that deserves to be nurtured: your friendship with yourself. In January 1993, I wanted a different sort of resolution for the year ahead. Instead of focusing on the usual, specific, gotta do stuff—get up earlier, walk thirty minutes, eat more fiber—I wrote down one simple goal. Three words that could be applied daily, as I saw fit. Words that would produce a changed life, which is really what we're looking for when we resolve to do something new.

Here is what I wrote:

Experience Beauty Daily

I know. You were expecting something . . . deeper, more significant sounding. But listen to what happened.

First, to give my phrase-for-the-year emphasis, I typeset it on my computer in a lovely, flowing typeface and printed it on pristine white paper. Then, taking a green ink pad and an ivy rubber stamp, I surrounded the words with colorful greenery and framed them in a silver, heart-shaped frame. (I felt like a third grader working on a school project, but what the heck . . . it was *fun!*) I placed the frame on the shelf in my bathroom, right next to the blow dryer and the velcro rollers.

Experience Beauty Daily. Each morning it hit me differently. Take an extra five minutes for a facial scrub and mask was one day's interpretation, and so I did. Pick fresh blackberries for breakfast was the thought that came to mind another morning. (Okay, Bill did the picking, but I ate them—out of an exquisite stoneware bowl.) Beautiful. Shave above the knee was yet another day's choice.

One morning, I spent ten indulgent minutes reading a favorite book that had nothing to do with work, child raising, or getting "buns of steel." It was just for enjoyment, just for me. Now on my third year of this method of motivation, I'm still experiencing something special each day (in 1994 it was Grace, in 1995, Peace.) Why is this simple reminder working, when all those to do lists over the years did not? Several reasons.. . .

1. There's plenty of room for creativity and no room for *should* or *must.*
2. The goal is experience, not perfection.
3. The measure of success is aesthetic, not numerical.
4. The reminder notice itself brings pleasure and a gentle, daily nudge in the right direction.

Sometimes we just need to encourage ourselves. I was delighted with the responses from women who have developed that strength of character that says, as Janet from Nebraska phrased it, "I'm okay the way I am." "I am not perfect, but there is nothing I want to change . . . right now!" admitted Sheila. Or, as JoAnne said, "Being forty, I finally like my character traits."

While we all long to remain flexible, if we've come to a place of peace and acceptance, the time for adapting and contorting may be over and the time for knowing and sharing our strength may be at hand.

14
Using the Sense(s) God Gave You

She perceives that her merchandise is good (NKJV).
She senses that her gain is good (NASB).
She sees that her trading is profitable (NIV).

Proverbs 31:18

We need all three translations to make sense out of this verse (pun intended). The "sense-ible" woman uses all five of her senses—sight, hearing, smell, taste, and touch—to determine if her labors and the fruits they produce are worth the effort. We've heard about women having a sixth sense, or intuition, but we are also called upon to use the five senses that God gave us more effectively to determine the profit of our efforts.

The Eyes Have It
Yogi Berra said, "You can observe a lot just by watching." Women watch everything but especially people's faces. We're looking for clues, for shades of meaning. We process all the visual messages, the body language, the facial language, the telltale signs of stress, fear, or anger. Some men are able to carry

on a conversation behind a newspaper. Women cannot. We have to watch others' faces while they speak to us; we want to look into their eyes to make sure we're communicating, no matter who is talking.

When she went back to school to become a nurse-practitioner, Cindy from Iowa "had to live two hours away, Monday through Friday for sixteen weeks, and my children were two and six at the time. When my daughter was playing with her doll house, I would watch as she put the family at the dinner table—Dad, brother, sister, but no Mom!" Instead, her daughter had the other doll sitting on the roof of the house. "Mom's at school," she explained.

Cindy reported, "I guess she adjusted to the situation pretty well after all. I'm happy to say that Mom is now sitting at the table with the rest of the family!" This wise mother could see for herself that her labor was neither in vain, nor did it have any long term ill effects on her family.

There are times, however, when we miss things that happen right before our eyes. Monica from Texas remembers when her grandfather passed away, and she and her eight-year-old daughter went to the funeral. The casket was open at the front of the church, and the two of them sat in a nearby pew, crying. While Monica was looking through her purse for a tissue, the casket was quietly closed and rolled to the back of the church. The young girl looked up first, noticed the casket was gone, and whispered to her distracted mother, "Where did Granddad go?"

Monica whispered as she blew her nose, "Honey, Granddad has gone to heaven to be with the angels."

Her wide-eyed daughter replied, "Man, that was fast! I didn't know they took the casket too!"

Do You Hear What I Hear?

When I ask my female audiences, "Do you think women hear better than men do?" the groan of agreement is deafening. We can all think of instances when men heard the words that were spoken, but *not* what was being communicated.

When Thanksgiving was supposed to be celebrated at our house a few years back, my in-laws kindly suggested we eat at a historic local restaurant on Thanksgiving Eve instead, so Bill and I could spend the long weekend working on restoring our new/old house. My guess is they also remembered another holiday at our house when it took me until 9:00 P.M. to get dinner on the table. In any case, off to that fancy restaurant we went on Turkey Eve to enjoy a delicious multicourse meal, with not one dish to wash. I was in heaven.

Near the end of dinner, Bill's dear grandmother, then in her early eighties, murmured softly, "Well, I don't know what I'm going to do tomorrow. Eat a turkey sandwich, I guess."

Driving home later that evening, I said, "Oh, Bill, we must never do this again. Nanny was so disappointed."

He looked at me in complete shock. "No, she wasn't! She said she was going to eat a turkey sandwich."

Did he hear the words? Every single one. Did he hear what she said? Not exactly. Women listen between the lines, between the words, for the tone, the energy, and the nuance of expression that really tell us what's being said. This isn't a fault-finding mission, just a fact-finding one: we women hear better. Most of the time.

Patty from Utah was confused when her four-year-old daughter came home from a friend's house, insisting that she wanted a zucchini.

"A what?" Patty asked.

"You know, like you wear when you go swimming. A zucchini!"

Then, there's the daughter who went home from Betty's class in North Carolina and told her mother, "I must have permission to take your slip to school tomorrow!" Sure enough, the next day, the child showed up at her teacher's desk carrying a brown paper bag with a pale pink size 38 undergarment inside, rather than what the teacher really wanted: a permission slip.

A Fragrant Aroma

And how well developed is our sense of smell? Bill buys me Estee Lauder's *Beautiful* perfume, not for his benefit, but for mine: I adore it. It's always under the Christmas tree, and to be a good steward, I make that bottle last a whole year. I get six squirts a day, then duck under the "fallout" to try and catch every little drop.

Women can always tell what fragrance their friends are wearing. "Oh, is that *White Shoulders*? Is that *Obsession*? Is that *Giorgio*?" We can "name that scent" with one whiff. On the other hand, if we extended a forearm featuring the six finest scents that a perfume department offered, some of our men would sniff their way past all six, get to our fingertips with the faint scent of onions from last night's dinner, and say, "Mm-m-m . . . that's delicious! Can you bottle that?"

I tried to wear an inexpensive musky thing one summer because I'd been too extravagant with my *Beautiful* all spring. The discount scent got tossed in the trash when Bill stepped into our bedroom right after I sprayed my sixth squirt of the cheap stuff and said, "Is that a new room deodorizer?"

A Matter of Taste

On the question, "Do men have as finely developed a sense of taste as women do?" it's tougher to get consensus. After all, there are famous male chefs the world over who do, indeed, have terrific tasters.

I can only go by my own limited, yet thorough, understanding of the American male taste buds that I have had to cook for over the years. That is to say, they ate my food, so they must have no sense of taste at all. Bill, bless his heart, will eat anything. We often have what at our house is affectionately called, "Chicken Done Some Tricky Way." These are boneless, skinless chicken breasts (aren't you proud of me?), done on the top of the stove in a non-stick pan with something thrown in for flavor. Could be mustard, could be ginger, could be honey, could be minced garlic, you just never know. For that matter, I never know. Which means if I hit on a really tasty combination, and Bill says, "This is wonderful! Can we have it again?" I have to be honest with him: "No. I'm not sure what it is." *And he eats it anyway.* File this under no taste or blind trust. Or maybe, true love.

Even Esther Didn't Wear Polyester!

What of our sense of touch? Consider two fabrics: 100 percent silk and 100 percent polyester. The first is ultra smooth, airy, liquid, floats on air, yet has a depth and texture all its own. The color and sheen, both dull and vibrant at the same time, are a dead giveaway. We can pass a woman at the mall, smile and say, "Lovely silk dress!" and she nods her thanks. Silk looks like nothing else but . . . silk.

Not to say that silk-like 100 percent polyester doesn't give it a valiant try. It, too, is smooth. A bit too smooth. Also light, but not quite the same sense of substance. Wonderfully washable and very tough, it has many qualities silk does not have, including the higher price tag. But we can tell, even with a glance, and definitely with a touch, which one is which.

Yet, if I hold up an expensive silk nightgown and a slinky polyester version for Bill to touch, he simply says, "Ooooh!" and wants to know how quickly I can slip into either one, bless him.

~ *She senses that her gain is good.*

The Sixth Sense: Intuition

So how should the perceptive woman utilize her five finely developed senses? Among other things, I use them to monitor my family carefully for signs of distress. Yes, my career is successful, but what effect does it have on my home life? This is not in any way to suggest that troubles at home stem from Mom going to work, of course. It's just our responsibility to perceive and assess and, sometimes, adjust. Working dads must do this too.

Using her eyes, ears, and heart, Leesa from Kentucky knows that the choices she has made for herself and her family were positive ones. After earning a five-year engineering degree and working for the government for three years, she retired to start her family. When her youngsters went off to school, they traveled in Mom's van, not the bus. Back and forth they went, day in and day out. "In the car," she said, "you have your kids' undivided attention. We have had many meaningful hours of conversation—about 1,800 hours in ten years! When we finally traded in our van, it had 158,000 miles on it." For Leesa, every mile was worthwhile. She "sensed that her gain was good."

Our children also use their five senses to assess the world around them. Donna Otto, author of *The Stay at Home Mom*, suggests that "there are three major qualities our children need to see in our lives: truthfulness in words or actions, faithfulness, and gratitude."[1] Her advice doubly suits the working mother, who must display those same three attributes at home *and* at work. Our children's eyes and ears are attentive in both arenas.

Sally from Indiana described the time her ten-year-old daughter was at home after school, waiting for both her working parents to get home.

> We had cautioned her to *never* tell anyone on the telephone that she was home alone, and that if anyone asked for one of us, she should reply, "Mommy/Daddy is in the shower." One day, a friend called and asked for me. My daughter dutifully replied, "Mommy is in the shower." Then the friend asked for my husband! Obviously we had failed to prepare her for this possibility. After thinking it over, she finally told the caller, "Daddy's in the shower with her."

Sally signed her story, "Living a kinky lifestyle in front of the kids!"

Sensory Overload

Even if I'm on hand during the after-school hours, I sometimes use the television as a convenient "keep 'em busy" tactic while I finish a project or start supper. Such shows or videos are chosen with great care because my eyes and ears tell me that most television is an utter waste of time for children. In fact, it's worse: it's a waste of *mind*. Dee Brestin, in *The Lifestyles of Christian Women*, commented that "television not only exalts the transitory and is blind to the eternal, but it saturates us with a flow of lies concerning how to be fulfilled."[2]

Instead, at our house we focus on shows that are positive, fun, creative, and share a good message. Initially, I was tempted to hide our television in a spare bedroom (or better still, in the barn), but a need to monitor every show made putting it right next to the kitchen in the family room the best choice for us.

As often as possible, we watch shows together—I'm a big kid at heart, anyway, so I enjoy all the animated programs. When things come up that are inappropriate, we turn them off and talk about why. I'm careful to say, "This is not healthy for *anyone* to watch," rather than, "You are too young to see this stuff." Matthew and Lillian, at five and seven, are still very compliant about my intervention. I intend to enjoy control as long as I've got it!

Recently, when a commercial for a very violent movie flashed on the screen and I hit the "off" button, I turned around to find Matthew diving to the floor, hands over his ears, saying, "I didn't look, Mom, I didn't look!"

Homeward Bound

In *The Woman Who Works, The Parent Who Cares,* coauthored with John Kelly, Sirgay Sanger, M.D., outlines what our children need from us and where we can focus our intuitive radar: "Security, trust, a sense of mastery and competence, humor, curiosity—all the qualities that matter to a child's future—originate not in what a woman does with her child but in how she does it; in other words, in the sensitivity of her interactional and relationship skills."[3]

Sometimes we don't trust our intuition, our sensitivity, or our mothering skills. Linda from Alaska wrote a lovely, long letter filled with wisdom for such among us:

I went to work when my kids were small because I couldn't stand being home and I didn't know how to properly run a household. When I was growing up, I was very much into my music and did not learn how to clean, cook, handle money, etc. I was in total shock when I married and had a home of my own. Work was an escape because I am a very organized person and had control and satisfaction at the office, unlike at home.

When I moved to Alaska, I had the opportunity to take a class on home organization from a woman who went from slob to totally organized. I discovered that I could run my home a lot like I ran the office, with time management, files, etc. Wow! What a discovery! I actually began to *love* caring for my home. Looking back, I would give anything to have known this information when my boys were small. I can plainly see that my life would have taken a different course, including that I probably would not have divorced my first husband.

I guess the bottom line is, please urge women who do not know how to care for their homes, and to whom it is important, to seek help! There are a number of excellent books, classes, videos, etc. It can be learned and it can be enjoyed!

Her words were echoed in the story of a woman who left her incredibly demanding newspaper career behind to reinvent home with her husband and five-year-old daughter. She realized that at last she had "put my house in order. What I'd feared the most, what had once looked like a huge, gaping void, gave me solace. In others words, my home life healed me."[4]

Falling in Love with Lillian

Interesting that her daughter was five when that healing occurred. For Miss Lillian's fifth birthday, I arranged a trip for the two of us to Disney World in Orlando. I'd taken her older brother there two years earlier when he was five; now, it was her turn. Just the girls, for two days. She talked of nothing else for weeks, which Matthew endured simply because it was, after all, only fair.

I was excited about the trip, too, but part of me was silently lamenting the sacrifice of time, of many precious hours I knew I should spend writing this very book, or preparing my summer speeches, or responding to some long past due correspondence. The financial sacrifice was real, too, since a day at the Magic Kingdom cost roughly the same as half a dozen of their classic videos. Oof.

Ready or not, the Big Day came and off, via Delta, we went. Without the need to compete for anyone's attention, Lillian was an absolute angel. She flirted with the pilots, entertained the passengers, and carried on a nonstop conversation with her stuffed pony, Brownie, who got the window seat. I was so proud of my little girl, who seemed to be growing up with each minute we were together.

Our first afternoon in Orlando, it was SeaWorld. My animal lover was beside herself with joy, watching Shamu and friends leap and splash. The next day dawned gray and rainy. "Not today, Lord," I thought, as Lillian and I climbed into our special new Disney World outfits. "Not the Magic Kingdom in a thunderstorm!"

Yup. There were no ponchos to be found for miles around, so a little fold-up umbrella was all we had between us and the monsoon. If I was worried that all the rain would dampen my daughter's enthusiasm (and I was), I hadn't counted on her amazing ability to go with the watery flow.

We did Dumbo the Flying Elephant in an absolute downpour, laughing all the way, then headed for dry land with two sailing trips through It's a Small, Small World, where every turn produced a "Wow! Look at that!" We fought a tempest in the Teacups and made our way through the Haunted Mansion with Lillian's head firmly buried in my chest. Big mistake, that one. Yet through it all, she was a trooper. With sheets of rain running down her face, she looked up at me, eyes sparkling, and said, "Mom, we're having a great time, aren't we?" Yes, dear one, we are.

◆ She sees that her trading is profitable.

The sun suddenly appeared for Mickey's 3:00 parade, and she wiggled and charmed her way up front and center to take it all in. I watched her shout with glee as the band came by, and found tears sneaking down my cheek. Oh, that pixie! So full of joy, such an unflagging spirit. By 7:00 that evening, she was finally running out of gas, and we made our way back to the hotel as the rains returned in earnest.

That night, fresh from her bath and wrapped in her cotton pajamas, she fell asleep instantly in my arms as we curled up for bed. I watched a movie, but mostly I watched Lillian: skin as smooth as satin, not a line or wrinkle; long lashes across her pink cheeks; curly dark blonde hair ringed around her sweet face. If you look up *cherub* in the dictionary, this is the face you see pictured there.

I had never felt such Mother Love as I felt that night, not just because she is beautiful (which, of course, she is!), and not just because she is clever and creative and charming, though she is those things too. At that precise moment, I fell in love with my daughter as if she were a long lost friend that finally had found her way to my door.

In her, I discovered my own childhood self, long buried; and in me, I found a new wellspring of love for precious little Lillian, and even for little Liz.

It was easy to use my five senses that day to perceive that the cost of this trip was money well spent, and that indeed, our "gain was good."

15

I Am Woman, Hear Me Snore

∼

. . . and her lamp does not go out by night.

Proverbs 31:18b NKJV

W e're talking about a real lamp here, the kind that the genie came out of in *Aladdin*. It's long and slender, with a handle, a spout, oil, and a wick. Apparently, the ideal woman literally left her lamp burning, long through the night.

My own mother did the same thing, except her lamp was a fluorescent kitchen light. She often stayed up after the dishes were done, playing solitaire to relax. She earned it, believe me. As a child alone in my big, upstairs bedroom, my five siblings already having flown the coop, I would take solace in the faint light that filtered up the stairwell. It meant Mom was awake and all was well. Later she confessed to me that she often left the light on and went to bed. Yet the light was there when I needed it.

So I come by my night owl tendencies honestly. Many a woman has found that after the kids and/or husband are tucked in bed, she finally has a peaceful moment to herself. As Julie from Kansas noted, "It's hard to cope when you feel you're always at the bottom of the list. Calgon, take me away!" A bubbly bath might be just the ticket, or a good read that puts our hardworking brains on Park for an hour, or some R & R time with hubby. The truth is, those late hours are when most of us finally get the chance to work without interruption. As one scholar phrased it, "she keeps her light burning at night in order to attain maximum production."[1]

Remember how early she started her day, rising while it is still dark? Now we know the truth: the night before was short too. And that's where we can get into trouble.

We call this pattern burning the candle at both ends. The '90s malady known as burnout comes from just such disregard for our body's genuine need for rest. Jill Briscoe cautions us that godly women are to "burn on, instead of burning out."[2]

How can we know when we're burning out? We find ourselves saying, "Nobody else can handle this but me," or "No one understands," or, after sheer exhaustion hits, "This is too much for me!" Of course it is; it's too much for any one woman. It would be like trying to actually do *all* the things described in Proverbs 31. Hm-m-m.

In her perceptive analysis of the problem of burnout in *Perfect Every Time,* author Paula Rinehart revealed that "some part of me felt that a calendar with empty spaces and a phone that didn't ring were proof of not being much in demand."[3] My eyes flew open like windows when I read that: that's me to the max!

For speakers, consultants, and other professionals whose success is indeed measured by how many spaces in the calendar are filled and how many times a day the phone rings, the potential for burnout is exceedingly high. Unlike the standard Monday through Friday, 9:00 to 5:00 sort of schedule, a small business owner can find herself filling up every one of those calendar spaces, week after week, month after month. I empathize completely with Paula's statement, "I tried to find the 'off' button inside me, but I couldn't reach the switch."[4]

Lots of us can identify with too-full calendars. Linda from Pennsylvania remembers one year when she got too busy:

Spring had rolled into fall and I had somehow never seen the summer. One day as I was rushing through the local supermarket, I saw a neighborhood woman who lived with her mother. "Hi, Alice!" I said. "How's your mother doing?" She looked at me, gasped, and said, "Linda, she passed away in July!" Embarrassed, I said, "Oh, I'm so sorry, I didn't know!" Again she looked at me, very perplexed, and said, "But Linda, you came to her viewing!" I realized then, it was time to slow down and smell the coffee!

Burning the Midnight Oil

Newspaperman Kin Hubbard wrote, "A bee is never as busy as it seems; it just can't buzz any slower." Some of us are still buzzing, but we can't move around as fast as we used to; furthermore, we aren't sure where the honeycomb is. The physical symptoms of burnout are easy to spot: crying, exhaustion, getting sick more easily and more often, losing our sense of humor, finding it hard to concentrate, becoming forgetful, always running late, wanting to sleep (or not being able to). Rinehart said, "I felt as though I were speaking through a plate glass window, and had someone possibly peeked around the edge, they would have found no one there."[5]

My friend Terry, who works at a local Christian radio station, once started his early morning show still dragging from the day before. The call letters of the station are "WJIE . . . Where Jesus Is Exalted." But that particular day, his first attempt came out, "WJIE . . . Where Jesus Is Exhausted"! Thank goodness all our overcommitments never truly wear *him* out. Yet, when we leave our light burning too long without trimming the wick, it can leave us with precious little of the oil of gladness.

One of my daughter Lillian's favorite toys is her pink plastic flashlight. She loves to climb into dark spaces and flash it on and off. However, if she neglects to turn it off and leaves it in a corner somewhere, shining away, it quickly wears the batteries down and the light goes out completely.

Pay attention, Liz!

I am always asked by friends and audiences alike, "How do you do it all? Be a mother, a wife, travel, write, run a speaking business . . . how?" Time was I would toss out a funny one-liner, like "Good drugs!" or "No sleep!" They weren't true statements, they were just funny.

Reality was not so humorous. I would slide out of bed at 4:00 A.M. and work until my family started waking up for breakfast, then join them at the table for a grand total of thirty minutes before they were off to school and office, where they would all remain for the next *eleven hours* while I worked feverishly in my home office. Finally, in the door they came, for hugs and homework and dinner (after a fashion), then I would slither out to the office for another hour of labor. Bath time gradually became Daddy's job, and I would show up for kiss and tuck-in time, another thirty-minute quickie. After lights out in the house, it was lights on in the office while I worked until midnight or 1:00 A.M. on some "gotta get it done now" project.

... and her lamp does not go out by night.

Occasionally, we all do that sort of thing. I received a letter recently from my fifty-two-year-old sister describing her latest wallpapering spree, in which she wrote, "The 2, 3, 4, and 5 A.M.s are catching up to me." Every now and again that kind of overtime activity is fun; it even feels rather daring. But as standard procedure, it can be deadly, if not to a body, perhaps to a marriage or any number of other vital relationships. As Lee from Wisconsin put it, "No matter how many balls we juggle, or how successful we look, we aren't always as we appear!"

I once overheard Bill explain to a mutual friend who had asked the familiar "How does Liz do it all?" question: "For Liz, sleep is an option." I smiled inside, thinking how amazingly productive a woman I was. The Bible calls that pride ... and it came before a fall, all right. Because my heart fell to my knees when I saw that Bill was not smiling when he said it. I wasn't just wearing myself out. I was wearing my beloved out too.

Time for a Change

Here is what happens when we work 80+ hours a week ("I love my job!"), don't get enough sleep ("Isn't four hours enough?"), get almost zero exercise ("What? Stop working to go for a walk?"), eat less than healthy foods at strange hours ("Oh boy! Pizza again!"), pop antacids like candy ("Where is that bottle of Extra Strength TUMS?"), and drink coffee like water ("Could you make a fresh pot?").

What happens is we lose all perspective, most of our friends, some of our hair and, eventually, all sense of meaning and significance in our lives. Carlysle said, "Nothing is more terrible than activity without insight." Not long ago, I realized that I had plenty of the first and none of the second.

The day comes when we find ourselves yelling at our kids, throwing stuff around the room, slamming doors, and screaming at anyone within earshot. If we have someone in our lives who loves us, we also may find ourselves walking through the door of a therapist's office.

Mother Teresa said it best: "To keep a lamp burning we have to keep putting oil in it." For those who are spiritually minded, that oil is the single most important ingredient in our lives. We can't manufacture the oil, we can't buy the oil, we can't even earn the oil. We just have to ask for it, so that we can burn brightly and clearly see the path ahead. "For Thou art my lamp, O LORD; / And the LORD illumines my darkness" (2 Sam. 22:29 NASB).

Therapy was the oil God used to relight my lamp. It is one of the best gifts I've ever given myself, even though I went through some of the worst days of my life to get there. The weeks that followed were no picnic, either. However, I rest in the truth of the old spiritual: "There is a balm in Gilead to make the wounded whole."

I am not the only one among the walking wounded, trudging through each day with little sense of purpose or passion and no clear view of the Big Picture anymore. We are legion. Consider the words of these women who offered an explanation of why they might want to seek more satisfying work, if not quit working completely:

"I would like to practice my profession—not manage papers."
Nurse for twenty-six years, age forty-six

"I feel unsatisfied and bogged down in monotony with no encouragement from my employer."

> Bookkeeper for twenty-one years, age forty-four

"The supervisors treat us like children."

> Telemarketer, age thirty-seven

"I feel unappreciated."

> Teacher for twenty-three years, age forty-four

"No job is worth all this incredible stress and time away."

> Nurse manager for twenty-six years, age forty-six

"I hate my job; too detail oriented, very little 'big picture.'"

> CPA for seven years, age forty-three

"After twenty-three years at one place, I'm tired of it."

> Nurse, age forty-two

"Enough already. Up every day, work all day, etc., etc."

> Marketing/PR for fifteen years, age thirty-eight

Do you hear your own voice among these? I don't on this day, but I sure have in the past, many times. You are worth taking care of, and there may never be a better time than this one to trim the wick and seek some fresh oil for your lamp.

In a book aptly titled, *Women's Burnout,* the authors offer a twelve-point checklist for avoiding burnout, including "avoid isolation," "learn to pace yourself," and "take care of your body." Number Twelve was my favorite: "Keep your sense of humor! Begin to bring joy and happy moments in your life. Very few people suffer burnout when they're having fun."[6]

The Paper Chase

We know laughter and a sense of play is what we need. It's also what we want more of in our lives, paired with less stress.

We Want More . . .	And Less . . .
Humor	Negativity
Play	Anxiety
Happiness	Sadness
Dancing	Eating
Laughter	Heartache
Serenity	Stress

If we do not choose to look for humor, believe me, it will look for us. One exquisite day in May, I had a luncheon program in Ocean City, New Jersey. After my presentation was over, the morning fog lifted and the oceanside resort was bathed in late spring sunshine . . . glorious! A wise and balanced woman would have given herself permission to take a stroll on the beach, but not this woman. No, I had work to do, a book to write, and no lollygagging allowed. My only concession to the beautiful day was to open the windows and invite the ocean breezes to gently fill the room.

Dutifully, I sat down with a huge file folder of papers and began to divide them carefully into ten neat piles: this goes in this chapter, that goes in that chapter. After four hours, my hard work neatly spread out before me on the bed, I got up to stretch and head out for an early dinner. Not a leisurely trip to a nice seafood restaurant—that would require *time!*—just a quick zip through the nearest drive-thru, then back to work.

Twenty minutes later, heading into the hotel with my paper sack dinner, I noticed the wind had picked up. Had I left those windows open? Hm-m-m. As I turned the key in the door and began to push it open, I noticed a strange "whooshing" sound and had a sense of the door opening on its own power. When the bed full of papers came into view, still in neat piles, I breathed a sigh of relief . . . until the door was fully open and a big gust of wind found a way of escape.

In seconds, nearly two hundred pages of notes were blowing everywhere, including through the door and down the hall.

"W-a-a-aaa!" came from my lips as I dropped my dinner sack and began chasing and stomping on runaway slips of paper.

A few minutes later, papers clutched willy-nilly in my hands, I made my way back to my room to survey the damage. The sea breeze had created a sea of papers, and all my afternoon labors had been in vain (the perfect word for it, since the word means, "a breath, a vapor"!).

I should've cried. I could've stamped my foot. I would've been justified in letting out one good scream. None of the above happened. I started to chuckle. Then a whole laugh sneaked out. Soon I was doubled over with laughter. I almost missed the bellman clearing his throat behind me as he held out a piece of paper with a bewildered expression on his face. "Ma'am? Did you lose something?"

Yes, I did. Thank goodness.

And I found something too. Annie Chapman, in *Smart Women Keep It Simple,* reminds us that in the Greek games, "The winner of the race was the one who came in first—with his torch still lit."[7]

16
Hands to Work, Hearts to God

**She stretches out her hands to the
distaff, / And her hand holds the spindle.**
Proverbs 31:19 NKJV

And you thought we were finished with wool and flax!
For those of us who haven't a clue about how a
spinning wheel works (including me), the distaff is
attached to the wheel and holds the flax. The spindle is the
hand-held rod on which the thread is wound as it's spun. Clear
as mud, I know.

It's hard for us almost-twenty-first-century women to glean much wisdom from an ancient method of spinning thread. But we can surmise two things:

1. **She was exceptionally skilled.** Why even mention it if spinning flax were not a skill coveted by mothers for their sons' future wives?

2. **It was a necessary and important task** for running both a home and a business. As we'll see later, the wool and flax that were spun on that wheel went into fabrics that clothed her family, and, by producing income, fed them as well.

We may not spin flax, but the women who filled out our surveys perform nearly every other job one could imagine. Among our ranks I found a private investigator, bill collector, research librarian, conference planner, stained-glass artist, math professor, school bus driver, art gallery owner, pharmacist, owner of a floor covering business, and one woman who was both an attorney *and* a flight attendant. What a mix of careers we have selected for ourselves!

Many times, women I meet almost apologize for their chosen field: "I'm just a teacher . . . just a secretary . . . just a nurse." Wait a minute. Education, clerical work, healthcare—those were the Big Three when I was growing up, careers of choice for a working woman in the '50s, '60s, and beyond. The work was, and is, difficult and, without a doubt, not as financially rewarding as it could and should be.

Yet these positions fit the above two stated criteria for our Proverbs woman—exceptional skill and definite need—perfectly:

Teachers are exceptional, and their work is the key to our future.
Thirty of the women who completed our surveys are teachers. My family is filled with teachers, from kindergarten through college. At last count, there were nine in my immediate family who are

in the business of changing lives through education, with more on the way. As more and more children at risk show up at school-house doors, the job of a teacher gets more difficult. Yet they persevere. I could not be more proud of them and of all of those among us who have dedicated themselves to the teaching professions.

Secretaries are gifted, and their skills are crucial to business.
Of those who responded to our surveys, more than 120 are secretaries. My years as a bookkeeper, a bank teller, and a receptionist taught me plenty about the business world and about life. My experience taught me that if the boss were out, no problem; the secretary knew everything. But if the secretary were out . . . run for the hills! Even though my paychecks were on the light side, I am proud of what I brought to those jobs and what many of us bring to our work in the clerical professions.

Nurses are highly trained and deeply committed to their vital jobs.
We heard from nearly one hundred nurses for our survey, plus fifteen women in other healthcare positions. Nearly half of my presentations these days are to healthcare audiences, some of the finest folks in the world. Many of us have entrusted our lives to nurses. These are the pros who keep their cool in a very stressful, life-or-death environment. They are continually learning new skills and technologies as they "stretch out their hands" to help a hurting world through the healing professions.

All this to say, the Big Three require great skill, much training, and are necessary to society's survival. No more "I'm just a . . ."! It's our job now as women to convince society of these truths, in order to bring the salaries of these professionals up to the level of their obvious competency.

What's in It for Us . . . Other Than Cash?

The Women's Bureau of the U.S. Department of Labor issued a national questionnaire in 1994: "Working Women Count!" They wanted to know, among other things, what we like best about our jobs. Which three would *you* check?

Good pay	Good coworkers
Good benefits	New skills
Flexible hours	Enjoyment
Training	Teamwork
Job security	Authority to make decisions
Productive work	

These are all valuable components of job satisfaction, certainly, but what I find interesting is that this list does not include the two things that most people—thousands of people from all over America, from all walks of life—have told me they want from their jobs, which are:

1. To create great products or provide superior service
2. To make a positive difference in the lives of others

The government's list is, sad to say, focused only on self: "what's in it for me?" Few potential employers would respond positively to an applicant walking in with the above long list of requirements, saying, "This is what you owe me." In our tough economy, employers are looking for team players who arrive with a list of skills and goals that they want to *bring* to the workplace, not that they hope to take from it. In the best work settings, bringing your best to your job *should* produce the kind of results you want as well. (We've all been around the block often enough to know this is not always the case.)

If we honestly expect management to focus entirely on making us happy, we will be sorely disappointed. Usually their efforts are aimed, first and foremost, toward creating a marketable product or service. This means that if we're looking for satisfaction from our work, we will need to look internally, not externally. George Bernard Shaw said, "This is the true joy in life: being used for a purpose recognized by yourself as a mighty one." Twenty-five years in the marketplace have taught me that Shaw is right, that true job satisfaction comes from knowing that you are the *best* person for the job and giving it your *best* shot every day. Not only for "them" but also for you.

Legend has it that after the death of John D. Rockefeller, someone asked his accountant, "How much did John D. leave?" The reply was brief: "Everything." When you're gone, few people will know or care how much money you made in your lifetime. But they will know if you made a difference.

Who Are Our Role Models?

Most of us have succeeded in the workplace because of specific individuals who mentored, encouraged, promoted, or demonstrated for us what it means to be a professional in our chosen field. Some of us learned, appropriately, from educators. Pat from Florida honored a teacher who "encouraged me to be more than I ever thought I could be." Pat from Michigan mentioned "three high school teachers who taught me to do the best job I could do the best way I could do it."

Many of us pointed to a particular boss or supervisor who showed us the path to professional achievement. Kathie said of her boss, "She adopted me (not on paper!)." Libby chose "a capable, yet feminine and kind vice president of administration." Sue has learned lots from her "general manager—she sees potential in everyone!" And Julie thinks highly of her boss, who is "comfortable with herself and accepts her limitations."

The biggest category for professional role models was our peers at work. Sylvia looks up to "my office mate—she's so balanced." Cindy admires "a nurse practitioner I work with," and Marilynn looks for encouragement from "my peers—they are givers." Gayle wrote glowingly of a coworker who is "spontaneous, encouraging, [and] good for my soul." And Christine respects those who work for her: "Some of the nurses on my staff embody *caring*."

Two things stood out as I studied the surveys: almost no one said, "This person helped me make more money," or "They gave me huge raises." The people we chose as role models in our work lives were people who cared, who were willing to go the extra mile, who gave freely of themselves.

The second thing I noticed was that, while the major women's magazines always list celebrities as the most admired women, real women like us chose each other, people who are not household words, do not make big bucks, and are not in the limelight.

 She stretches out her hands to the distaff, / And her hand holds the spindle.

The only celebrity acknowledgment listed on the eight hundred surveys I read was a tip of the hat to Eleanor Roosevelt by Terry from Pennsylvania: "She was a *worker*, futuristic in her thinking and generous with her time." Even in this case, it was Eleanor's heart for service, and not her money or fame, that impressed Terry.

Mothering Is a Profession Too

I've always nodded with understanding when I see the T-shirts that proclaim, "Every Mother Is a Working Mother." Truer words were never said. I have to fight the urge to laugh when I hear younger women say, "I'm going to stick with this job until I'm thirty, then quit working and have children." "Don't worry," I say, smiling, "you'll still be working!"

Mothering definitely embodies the two job criteria mentioned earlier—exceptional skill and definite need—with a special definition of the word *labor-intensive*. Deborah Fallows, author of *A Mother's Work,* wrote, "At its best, work can offer a kind of spiritual satisfaction—a special feeling of achievement, a special wholeness, a sense that it is worthwhile, important, irresistible. This is the lesson about work from which women at home should draw."[1] She is so right. All work, done well, has value, regardless of the size, or existence, of a paycheck.

One thing the surveys demonstrated clearly: our parents are often role models for us, which means we may be the role models of choice for our children. Now, *that's* a scary thought! Our kids are watching us more closely than we can imagine as they make decisions about the value of work, both in and out of the home. I, for one, believe they deserve a good show.

When the kids see my suitcase at the door or find me all

dressed up in pantyhose and heels, they know I'm off to give a speech. (Believe me, I don't wear pantyhose unless absolutely necessary, since putting them on qualifies as an aerobic activity!) Because I have such an excellent track record for returning home within a day or so, the children seldom display any misery about Mother leaving. In fact, for years they thought I spoke at the airport. After all, that's where they would drop me off and pick me up. They probably decided that I simply rode to the top of the escalator and spoke to anyone who would listen! So when they see the heels and hose, Matthew gives me his biggest smile and says, "Mama . . . have a good speech!" I am fully aware that this enthusiasm may not last much longer, but I am enjoying every minute of it.

When I land at the airport the next day and run into their waiting arms (which sometimes are waiting for me at home), what do you suppose Matthew asks me right away? "Mama . . . did you have a good speech?"

Now what am I going to say to that angel of a boy? "No! I just showed up, put in my time, collected my check, and left." Obviously not. He deserves better than that, and so do my audiences. It is my goal each time to be able to come home and look my children in the eyes and say, with a clear conscience, "Mama did her best."

My high school drama coach used to say, "There are no small roles, only small actors." Whatever role God has given us to play out on the stage called life, we need to stretch out our hands and grasp the spindle, the chalk, the telephone, the computer, the thermometer, the microphone, and go for it. Without apology. Without compromise. Without giving less than our best because the money could be better or because we'd rather be somewhere else. Our children, our husbands, our parents, our friends, our peers, and our role models are in the audience . . . let's take a bow!

17
Reaching beyond Ourselves

She extends her hand to the poor, /
Yes, she reaches out her hands to the
needy.

Proverbs 31:20 NKJV

*A*n excellent woman not only stretches out her hands
to spin thread, she also stretches beyond the walls of
her home to meet the needs of the less fortunate. Our
pastor once said, "Maturity means growing less self-centered
and more other-centered."

Nancy from Illinois and her husband are other-centered. They
saw a need for a good preschool that also offered before- and
after-school care and summer day camp for children of working
parents. So, they built a nonprofit facility, financed in part with
their own dollars. Nancy wrote, "We both work hard and are not
rich. Our commitment to each other and this project has made
us very close. We cut out a lot for our family to make this project
go for our community."

This family's need for material goods is apparently balanced
out by the intangible good they receive. According to The
Institute for the Advancement of Health, "People who volunteer
regularly—at least once a week for two hours—are ten times
more likely to be in good health than people who don't. Benefits

range from an increase in their overall sense of well-being to a decrease in stress-related problems." By sharing her "filled hands," as the Amplified version says, an excellent woman in turn receives a full heart. I've never known anyone who volunteered time, talents, or money who walked away empty-handed.

Help! Not "One More Thing!"

My heart's desire is to find more opportunities to give myself away and teach my children the joy of service at the same time. One little problem: *when?!* A friend of mine once moaned, "There's just not enough of *me* to go around." Lots of us feel the same way and can't bear the thought of adding one more activity, one more to do item to our list, however worthy it may be.

For busy women like us, who don't know how we could manage the added role of volunteer, psychologist Virginia O'Leary offers a word of encouragement: "The more roles women have, the better off they are, and the less likely they are to be depressed or discouraged about their lives. When we have a lot to do, we complain that it's driving us crazy—but, in fact, it's what keeps us sane."

It's ironic that one of the best remedies for impending burnout is to give yourself away. To pick one time and place each week where you stretch out your hands for the pure joy of doing it. Not to earn brownie points or extend your professional network, but just to give something away, for their sake and your sanity.

What usually suffices for giving around our house is Mom writes a check. Sure, a generous one, but still it's only paper. Our angelic role model from Proverbs didn't stretch out her wallet—let's face it, that's often the easy way out—she stretched out her hands and got involved in the lives of her needy neighbors. The studies on the benefits of giving are clear on this: It is the sacrifice of our time and talents that produces results for both parties, something the sacrifice of our dollars alone can't accomplish.

Not that financial gifts don't have their merit. As the Amplified Bible states, "She reaches out her filled hands..." Since Lemuel was King, he was also wealthy, so the ideal wife for him would've been generous with their riches. She knew that their prosperity was to be shared not hoarded. "To whom much is given, from him much will be required" (Luke 12:48 NKJV).

A family I know in Louisville keeps a big, clear jar on the kitchen table to collect all the excess change everyone has in their pockets at the end of the day. When the jar is full, the family chooses an appropriate charity to receive their gift. It's simple but very effective, and each one gets to "stretch out their hands," not just Mom.

A Chinese fortune cookie recently told me that "generosity and perfection are your everlasting goals." Not quite accurate. I'll leave perfection to the angels, and keep generosity as my target.

Stretching Out

Paul from Kentucky offered some words of wisdom to all of us who feel called to share our abundance with others. He said, "We can have our cake and eat it, too . . . but please, let's chew with our mouths closed and never talk with our mouths full!" We need to remember his good counsel when we are offering encouragement to someone whose life is not a piece of cake, whose burdens are heavy and needs are many. It's imperative that we not rub it in about how good we may have it (for the moment!), but instead be sensitive to the situations others find themselves in and give as generously as we can.

Something we found in the surveys caught me by surprise. Several women said they wanted to quit their jobs but *not* primarily to be home with family *or* to take a much-deserved break. No, they wanted to give their time away! As MeLynda from Utah phrased it, "I have enough volunteer work to keep me busy into the next life." And, when asked what they wanted more of and less of in their lives, some women wanted "more money to help the ones who really need it" and "more time to help others."

Shirley from Illinois "extends her hands" on the job every day but insists she gets back much more than she gives. Her advice to us? "Don't ever pass up the opportunity to visit with residents of a nursing home. It will be a day you'll never forget. There is so much love and joy in their hearts, and you can learn so much from them, just by sitting and talking. In fact, it will become addictive!" There's one addiction we won't need a cure for.

She extends her hand to the poor, / Yes, she reaches out her hands to the needy.

A dozen years ago, my first friend in faith, Evelyn, taught me a valuable lesson about being generous. She and her husband Tim did the morning show at the same radio station where I was doing the midday program. While I came to work at the reasonable hour of 8:00 A.M., they had to show up no later than 5:00 A.M. At that hour, they had to walk through a back alley and pass our big dumpster to enter through the back door. One morning, they found a woman with a grocery cart and ragged clothes digging in the dumpster for something to sell or eat. Evelyn offered her some money, but the woman shot her a nasty look and said, in effect, "I don't need your money!"

Ev knew better, of course, but didn't want to destroy this woman's pride. So the next morning they came to work a few minutes earlier so Ev could stuff cans of food all through the dumpster, hoping they would look like they were accidentally thrown away. Sure enough, when they came out later that morning after their show, the cans were gone. I've heard of collecting canned goods for the needy, but Evelyn took that idea one step further!

A Friend in Need . . .

Speaking of friends, there are times when they need our "filled hands" too. Or our "empty ears." A 1993 Louis Harris survey indicated that some 60 percent of us have between two and ten friends, and nearly 18 percent insisted they had more than twenty friends. Must have been men. Men could easily know twenty guys they think of as buddies, people they work with, hang out with, and so forth. But twenty close friends? The experts say you can only maintain three to five intimate friendships at any one time. My own definition of a *real* friend is someone you can call and sob, "It's me!"—at 3:00 A.M.—and they don't hang up on you! Or say, "Who is this?" Instead they say, "I'll be right over."

My friend Janie Jasin once said, "I believe everyone around us is needy and that we can truly minister to them only when we are fairly well ourselves." The people in our circles of influence are seldom in need of food or clothing, although such people exist by the millions and deserve all the help we can provide. But the deeper, greater needs of people often go unspoken, yet can clearly be heard by those with listening hearts.

"Liz, how many grandmas are out there in situations similar to mine?" asked a woman named Mary. Her daughter has returned home with two toddlers in tow and no money, so Grandma is raising a second generation while her daughter goes to school. She wrote, "If this is where God has me, then I'll just 'bloom where I'm planted' although I sure do wilt quickly!"

Nancy had a simple request: "Let me know that even though I failed in my marriage, I'm still an okay person." Definitely okay. Another woman submitted three funny stories about her family life, but it was the handwritten note at the bottom that slid through my heart like a dagger. "Liz, I have recently gone through a real painful divorce. My husband of twelve years left me for a woman half his age. He's put the girls (five and seven) and me through some real hurt, and we're still not settled due to his greed. Please pray for us!" Consider it done.

The truth is, the needy are all around us. Like the Proverbs 31 woman, we can stretch out our hands and find those who need our healing touch waiting right at the ends of our fingertips. A kind word, a nod, a squeezed hand can keep them going (and meet our own neediness as well).

Putting It All in Focus

At a recent presentation I gave for cancer patients and their families, one young woman told me, "Cancer really puts life in focus for you, and prioritizing gets easy." Dauna, whose young daughter was battling cancer, offered these words of wisdom: "Every single holiday after a cancer diagnosis is more meaning-ful. Christmas is merrier, birthdays become more important than a national holiday, and Thanksgiving comes 365 days a year."

My presentation for those cancer patients, by the way, was on the benefits of *humor* for both the survivor and the supporter. Surprised? They were wonderful laughers, and they especially appreciated the story of Gilda Radner, who fought ovarian cancer to the end by using her best weapon: humor.

When it was time for Gilda's first radiation treatments, she did all the necessary reading and brought her last three questions on 3" by 5" cards:

1. "What are the possible side effects?"

2. "How do I treat them?"

3. "Do you validate for parking?"[1]

Monica from Pennsylvania declared that "every bad happening has some good in it." When her husband was struck by a speeding car a few years ago, she realized that "in thirty years of marriage, Andy and I never found time to say 'I love you' to each other. We now say it 100 times a day, no matter how busy we get!"

Each of these stories is a gentle reminder that the needs around us—whether financial, practical, emotional, or spiritual—are many. We can't meet all those needs, but we can do something. For our own sake as well as theirs.

After hearing me present a program in her town, Dorothy from Iowa wrote a letter of encouragement telling me "how wonderful it was to share a happy day with you." Then she revealed a bit of her life's journey with me: when she was eight, her parents divorced; at fourteen, she had to quit school and go to work; at fifteen, she married a man "who loved me very much," and together they had six children before her husband's death at the young age of forty-nine; three of her six children suffered traumatic illnesses; she was recently diagnosed with Chronic Fatigue Syndrome, and her seven-year-old grandson has cerebral palsy. She closed her letter, "Sending my love and prayers for your happiness."

And for yours, Dorothy. You've reminded me, and perhaps many others, of how little we have suffered on this earth compared to many. How humbling, even embarrassing, to think of the little things we've complained about, when we should be on our knees in gratitude for all that has been given to us.

Forgive me, Lord, for not grasping the real definition of *needy*: someone who keeps her full hands in her pockets and misses the joy of stretching them out.

18

Let It Snow,
Let It Snow . . .

When it snows, she has no fear for her
household; for all of them are clothed
in scarlet.

Proverbs 31:21 NIV

I've spent my Christian life trying to live up to the woman described in Proverbs 31, but when it comes to this verse, I'm left out in the cold. Could it be she's not worried about her family being out in the snow because they're all dressed in bright red so she won't lose track of them against the white backdrop? Not quite. "Scarlet" was the best cloth available, a doubly thick fabric that kept her family warm on cold winter nights.

"How Cold Was It?"

Growing up in eastern Pennsylvania, I saw my share of bad winters, so neither snow nor cold struck fear in my heart. Until January 1994, when Louisville had the biggest snowfall on record—ever—an amazing sixteen inches. The next day we had the coldest temperature on record—ever—right at twenty-four degrees below zero. Or as the TV meteorologist cheerfully phrased it, "Fifty-six degrees below freezing!"

The kids were bouncing off the walls, anxious to go out and play in all that white stuff, but cautious Mother kept looking at the thermometer and saying, "No way!" By the third day, the snow hadn't budged an inch, and we'd been stuck in the house together for seventy-two solid hours. I was ready to let the kids out, period, cold or no cold. As our minister said the following Sunday, there was absolutely *no* crime that week in Louisville, but domestic arguments were way up!

More than anything, the kids wanted to make snow angels. I dressed them up as if they were embarking on the Iditarod and followed them out into the snow. *Note:* Do not let a five-year-old lie down in sixteen inches of snow to make an angel. *Angelic* is *not* how she behaved when all that snow and cold made its way into her boots and mittens. After spending nearly an hour locating all our winter paraphernalia, I think we stayed outside a grand total of twelve minutes.

One Ohio mother remembers "a series of wintry, blowy, snowy days" when her three children were suffering from cabin fever and "were absolutely out of sorts." After dressing them from head to toe, she sent them outside with strict instructions to walk around the house three times, "while I ran from window to window to make certain they were all still alive and still moving!"

Reminds me of the story my father-in-law tells of a little girl in Lexington who announced to her family that she found out why ice looks just like glass. "The weatherman said there's a *windshield factory* out there!"

Spectacle on Ice

The Proverbs woman wasn't worried about snow because she was ready for that nasty weather. We, on the other hand, were *not* ready for sixteen inches of snow and were caught with our mittens off. It was weeks before the snow and ice finally disappeared, but we were soon back to business as usual in my office behind the house.

Most of our books, tapes, and toys are stored there, but one product item was so big it had been exiled to the barn: 5,000 bright red kazoos packed in ten huge cardboard boxes. Luckily, kazoos don't melt or rust or attract silverfish. I mean really, what would a silverfish do with a kazoo? So they were perfectly safe in the drafty old barn, though hardly convenient when needed.

Naturally, we ran out of our office supply of kazoos the week after the Big Storm. Since I'm the boss, it was my job to get a fresh box. "I hope you all appreciate this!" I grumbled, yanking the door shut behind me. I stomped through the snow to the barn, only to discover that the steep ramp that led up to the doorway was covered with ice. No problem. By reaching up and grabbing the door handle, I managed to pull myself up the slippery ramp, shove open the door, and fall into the barn. There! Made it.

Once my eyes adjusted to the dim light, I found a box of kazoos, brushed off the dust and cobwebs, and made my way back to the doorway. Now the same ramp that had posed no challenge going up, on the down slope looked like some maniacal amusement park ride: "Terror on Ice."

"I'll just put my feet sideways and slide down," I thought, and off I went. For the first few seconds, it felt like an exhilarating ride on a skateboard. "Whee!" I called out. Then, the gravity of the situation swept over me, and my round bottom headed south. The kazoos flew north. My legs went east and west, respectively. A shriek hung in the frozen air like a large icicle suspended from a tall branch.

Ka-thwomp! All points converged at the foot of the ramp,

where kazoos, round bottom, and both legs were reunited. I ran a quick body check for broken bones and, finding none, replaced the frozen shriek with the warm, toasty sound of human laughter. Just my own, thank goodness.

Gathering up the box of kazoos and what was left of my dignity, I marched through the snow toward the office, head held high. I had survived, and for that I was grateful, if not graceful. Besides, my staff would never know about my slippery trip, I thought, breezing through the door. Their burst of laughter told me differently. "Liz, there's a big, muddy circle on the back of your coat!" My body may not have been "clothed in scarlet," but my face was.

Yes, Bucky, There Really Is a Santa Claus

Snow means winter, and winter means Christmas, which means with children, there's always the issue of Santa Claus. One afternoon close to the holidays, Beverly from Tennessee came home to find her then six-year-old son very upset. "Mom, Bobby said there is no such thing as Santa Claus!" he said. "He did?" she said, sounding surprised. "Well, what did you say to him?" With great conviction, her son replied, "I told him there was so a Santa Claus because my mother would never spend that much money on me!"

In the Buckeye State some years back, another two young boys who were checking on Santa's status got themselves in a heap of trouble. Kelly had two sons, eighteen months apart. "The oldest, Scott, was the leader of most of the anarchy around our house. Unfortunately, the second son, Bucky, was usually a willing follower."

Christmas 1975 dawned with the usual 6:00 A.M. alarm. But when Kelly stepped into the living room "an incredible sight met my eyes. Shreds of wrapping paper, ribbons, and tissue were piled to the ceiling. Opened gifts for grandparents, aunts and uncles, cousins, friends, everybody, littered the room. It was a horrifying sight. Thoughts of all the time I had spent wrapping and curling ribbon swam through my mind, as well as the awful realization I would have to do it all again before lunch. I had to remind myself that murder was against the law."

The dialogue with her six-year-old son, standing amid the ruins, went as follows:

Kelly: "Oh, Bucky! How did this happen?"

Bucky: (get ready, he had quite a lisp) "Well, Thcott thaid, 'Letth go down and thee if Thanta came yet.' We came downthtairs and then Thcott thaid, 'Leth jutht open one gift.' Then we wotht contwol."

Twenty years later Kelly admits she almost "lost control" herself. "I thought my holiday was ruined. Now it's one of the few Christmases that I specifically remember, other than the one when the tree fell over."

Which brings us to Sandy from Pennsylvania:

When I was a child, my father always required us kids to hang each piece of silver tinsel perfectly straight, perfectly spaced on the Christmas tree boughs. For twenty years of my married life I never used tinsel on the tree, afraid Daddy might criticize my results. The year he died, we pulled out an antique box of tinsel and "threw" it on the tree, saying "Daddy, this is for you!" It was so much fun!

That Christmas morning, we were relaying the tinsel story to our many assembled guests when all of a sudden, with no one near the ten-foot tree, it fell onto the floor without breaking one ornament. Mother spoke first. "Well, your father always *did* have the last word!"

O Tannen-bomb!

In our own family, every Christmas is identified by one specific memory—the Christmas I made smoked turkey without meaning to, the year I gave everyone their gifts in brown paper bags with bows drawn on them, the Christmas Day we spent on the Pennsylvania Turnpike. But 1992 will always be remembered as the year I spoke our Christmas tree into existence.

I don't mean like, "And then God said, let there be . . ." I mean

I gave a speech for a charitable organization, and my honorarium was a ten-foot Christmas tree, decorated from top to bottom.

Usually we made a trip to a nearby tree farm and cut our own fragrant spruce. But that year, a ready-to-go artificial tree was a welcome gift since we were in the process of moving to our new/old house. Tree cutting had been pushed aside by painting, papering, and unpacking, and besides it might have taken weeks to find the ornaments. I was thrilled at the thought of receiving our "free tree."

When Bill's parents and grandmother arrived for our traditional bowl of homemade soup and bread, we hurried them in to see our tree. "It's lovely!" my mother-in-law exclaimed. "It was free," my son Matthew declared proudly. Like his father, he appreciates a good bargain.

Our first Christmas in the old house with the new tree went without a hitch. When New Year's Day came, traditionally the day for taking down a cut Christmas tree and sweeping up the dried needles, I came to a wonderful "aha!" realization: this tree would never lose its needles. I could enjoy it right through Epiphany.

By mid-January, still cozy in one corner of the dining room, the tree continued to look fresh and green, though a tad off-season. I removed all the yuletide ornaments and left only the twinkling lights and white snowflakes on the branches. "It's a January tree," I informed the family, and there the tree stayed.

When February came along, it seemed appropriate to replace the snowflakes with valentines, so the kids and I had a ball covering the tree with paper hearts. Not every family has a valentine tree, I thought warmly.

Frankly, the shamrocks in March got lost amid all the green, so on the first of April we moved quickly to Easter eggs of every hue and multicolored grass dripping from the branches. It was my favorite month so far.

Friends were less impressed. When my in-laws came for Easter dinner, they took one look and said, "Well!" I said, "It's an Easter tree," and they said, "Yes, it is."

By May it was getting harder to keep the branches dust-free and, though lovely, the sunflowers couldn't overcome the

Christmas-in-July look. Visitors would roll their eyes, and even the kids were weary of explaining to people that "Mom thought it would be fun to have a holiday tree all year."

By August, it was history: a two-piece memory shoved back in the corner of the garage. November rolled around, and it was time for my annual holiday presentation for that very charitable organization. With a request for my speaking services came their generous offer: "Liz, may we give you another tree again this year?"

"No thanks," I said. "I'll take a wreath."

The Reason for the Season

There were years when I didn't even have a Christmas tree, those single adult years through my twenties and early thirties when money was tight and a tree-for-one didn't sound like much fun. Usually, I worked Christmas day. Radio stations are an every-day-of-the-year kind of business, so rather than let my married friends work and miss time with their families, I always volunteered to do the morning show on Christmas. (Don't be impressed . . . I also got paid double-time!)

It was December 25, 1984, and there I was on Christmas morning, standing in the studio, the only person in the building other than a security guard and a news reporter. I was feeling very sorry for myself—all alone, no phone callers, no visitors, just me spinning carols and hymns on the turntables while big tears ran down my cheeks.

"Nobody loves me, Lord!" I said aloud in my most forlorn voice. "Nobody loves me!" I was sobbing by this point, feeling the most alone I'd ever felt in all my life. Then I heard his voice speaking to my heart as clearly and distinctly as the words on this page: "I love you, Liz. I love you."

My response was immediate and instinctive; I dropped to my knees. What love is this, that he would speak to me, his child, on Christmas morning! At that moment, the words of the music blasting out of the studio speakers penetrated my heart: "Joy to the world! The Lord is come!"

He came to us then, he comes to us now, and his message is still the same: "Have no fear of the cold. I love you!"

19

Step Aside, Laura Ashley

She also upholsters with finest tapestry.

Proverbs 31:22 TLB

I can handle a woman who sews her own clothing. With the help of Simplicity and a good zigzag sewing machine, even an inept seamstress like me can crank out something to wear—maybe not in public, but wearable. But here we have a woman who "makes for herself coverlets, cushions, and rugs of tapestry" (AMPLIFIED BIBLE). Now, that's a house of a different color!

Growing up in a small town nestled among Amish farmlands, I had only one friend whose mother was employed. She worked for an upholstery shop, and she was amazing. Old couches turned into beautiful, new-looking sofas under her able hands. Pillows got plump again, and drapes were created to match the upholstery. I was in awe of her powers with needle and thread and mighty machine.

But when Proverbs was written, Elias Howe had not yet ushered in the sewing machine age. So our magnificent woman from centuries ago not only created the thread, not only wove it into fabric, but she also hand-stitched her exquisite tapestry into fine coverings for her home. It makes me tired to think about it.

One might decide that this Queen of Upholstery was a figment of Lemuel's imagination, except I know her twentieth-century counterpart. One Saturday morning I phoned my friend Doris, whose name brings to mind the biblical seamstress Dorcas. "Whatcha doin'?" I asked. "Oh, I just bought some fabric this morning, and I'm going to cover my couch," she said.

I stifled my laughter. "Get serious!" I said. "I am serious," she assured me. And she was. She covered a queen-size sofa bed in one day. Six pillows. Arm covers. Scary.

Inferior Design

It's not that I don't adore home decorating. That love affair began at the dawn of puberty when I turned twelve and my two older sisters had vacated our big bedroom. Mother decided I was old enough to choose a new decorating scheme myself. Did I do a safe pale blue, a feminine pink, a slightly daring lavender? No, I went for a Mother Nature look: navy blue walls (think sky) with *bright* yellow floral wallpaper on the ceiling (sun), brown painted floors (dirt) with green throw rugs (grass, of course). And to think Earth Day hadn't even happened yet. I was ahead of my time. Way ahead of my time.

Mother, being a gardener, thought it was dandy. She even helped me antique the desk and bookshelf—remember that look? We used yellow paint for the base color then brushed on dark blue stain and wiped half of it off. It looked as bad as it sounds: green and yellow striped furniture. My friends made gagging sounds when they walked in the room.

I've traveled the interior design highway many times since then. My first apartment furniture consisted of one metal pole shelf earned with S & H Green Stamps and a dreadful plaid sofa bed bought with a credit card. Next came the early '70s hippie look with oversized floor pillows in earthtone colors: tans, browns, and rust. (Did we really decorate with olive and orange?) Stores sold huge pillows for hundreds of dollars, but penny-pinching apartment dwellers like me went the homemade route, creating enormous pillows that took up lots of empty floor space.

I bought remnant fabric for a song, and ordered loose foam rubber by the fifty-pound bag, which I had to tie on top of my car just to get home. You haven't lived until you've watched a 5'9" woman stuff a 7' by 7' pillow—from inside the pillow. The foam rubber pieces created their own static electricity after a while and insisted on sticking to my clothes and hair. Exasperated, I finally locked all the doors, pulled down the shades, took off all my clothes, put on a shower cap, and stuffed my floor pillows in the nude, hoping no one would ask me how I spent my weekend.

"What did you do Friday night, Liz?"

"Well, I peeled off all my clothes and climbed into a pillow."

"Naked?"

"That's right. Cuts down on the static electricity."

Since the pillow years, I've limited my adventures in sewing to curtains. One casing, one hem, hang it up—that's my speed.

Playing with Blocks

The other mainstay of the struggling-college-student apartment was the bookshelf: long pine boards on cement blocks. So attractive. I had lots of books and lots of records and lots of stereo equipment, so I naturally needed lots of cement blocks. At thirty-two cents each, I thought they were the deal of the century. The man at the quarry looked at me sideways when I pulled up in my '67 Volkswagen and ordered twelve large blocks. "In that car?" he asked. "No problem, I've got plenty of room in the back seat!" I assured him, jumping out.

One by one, he lugged the large, gray blocks over to the car and heaved them into the back. I wondered why he wasn't carrying two or three at a time. They looked so light, what with the two holes in the middle and all. They couldn't be that heavy. But as each one disappeared into the back of the Bug, the tires sank lower and lower. "Better put some up front," he advised, dropping the last two in the passenger seat. I happily paid him his $4.00 and headed for home, proud of my bargain-bookshelf-to-be.

I lived on a steep hill. I lived on a second floor. Parking by the curb, I whipped open the passenger door and grabbed the first cement block with one hand, just like the guy at the quarry had. It didn't budge. The steep downhill slant of the street meant I had a double fight with gravity. With two hands and a big grunt, I got the block onto the sidewalk. Good grief, I thought, this job will take an entire hour. Another "oof!" and we made it to the grass. I continued with an end-over-end tumble move to get it to the front steps. I looked like an unhappy hippie doing the Watusi with a cement block.

Finally, there was no getting around it. I had to pick up the block and march up those steps. Seven steps on the outside of the house, a twenty-step staircase on the inside. Circular.

The fact that I am alive to write this book means I survived, but I don't know how. It took an entire afternoon of huffing and puffing to get those dozen cement blocks up to my apartment. I knew then that I would have to seek more fruitful employment so that I could afford movers so that I would never, ever have to touch those blocks again. They traveled with me for five more apartments in four more states, and indeed, I never "oofed!" again.

In the Pink

When it came to decorating, I found my best bet was paint. It was inexpensive, came in a zillion colors, and required no sewing, stuffing, or hauling. There wasn't any shade I wasn't willing to try: dark green, paper bag brown, turquoise, even feldspar.

Feldspar? The dictionary will tell you it's something found in igneous rocks, but I'm telling you this is *not* a color found in nature. Picture the deepest, brightest coral imaginable, then multiply it by ten. That's feldspar: a color one should use in *very* small doses, which is why it seemed the perfect choice for my tiny, 6' by 7' laundry room.

Never one to rush such projects, I waited until the night before the delivery men would arrive with my new washer and dryer to start painting. How long could one little room take? Anyway, the hardware store insisted it would cover in one coat. I popped open the can and gasped. Feldspar my foot, this was flamingo pink! With trepidation, I poured it into the paint tray and was soon rolling it onto the walls.

Flat and vertical, the color was more coral than pink, and I sighed with relief as I rolled and trimmed, rolled and trimmed. By 1:30 A.M., I had finished three walls and was pleased with the progress, except for one minor point: it was going to take two full coats to cover the old paint. Filling up the paint tray for the last wall, my tired arms stretched the tray up onto the shelf that perched on the side of the ladder.

Maybe it was the late hour, the lack of sleep, or too many paint fumes, but my next move was a terrible one: I moved the ladder. The forgotten paint tray, filled with a quarter of a gallon of bright pink latex, came raining down on my horrified head. If my mouth had been hanging open as usual, I might have drowned. Instead, the metal paint tray landed right on my chest, cascaded paint down the front of my T-shirt and jeans, and landed with a clang at my feet.

Now, the good news: for the first time in my natural life, I had used a drop cloth. On previous painting expeditions, I'd taken one page of newspaper and scooted it around the room with my foot, painting as I went. But because this laundry had a nice hardwood floor, I had wisely covered it with a vinyl drop cloth, a fact that at that moment gave me great solace: it could have been worse.

Had I been a married woman then, I would've called out, "Honey!" and some kind man would've come to my rescue. But I was a single woman when I bought that house, and the only other creature under my roof was my large cat, now perched on the laundry doorstep, looking mighty curious.

I know what most of us would've done: we would've stopped right then and there and gotten ourselves all cleaned up before continuing. But I was not about to waste all that paint, and anyway I had a job to finish. So, I stepped up to the fourth wall and smeared myself all over it, trying to make use of every drop of feldspar on my body. By this point, the clothes were a write off, so I wiggled out of them, turned them inside out and dropped them in the trash can. (I know what you're thinking: does she always do her decorating projects in the buff? No, but when you live alone, you can get away with a lot!)

It was now 2:00 A.M., the first coat was complete and would have to dry for two hours before the second coat could be applied. Certainly at this point a sane woman would have taken a moment to jump in the shower and wash off all that pink paint, but it seemed so pointless. In two hours, I'd be back into the mess all over again, I reasoned, so I simply pulled back the comforter on my bed, pulled back the sheets, pulled back the mattress pad, and positioned myself on top of the mattress. The paint had only landed on my front half, remember, and it was completely dry by now, to boot.

I set the alarm for 4:00 A.M. and immediately fell into a deep sleep. Two hours later, I woke up on the first ring, rolled and trimmed with feldspar abandon, then showered and dressed for the day and was drinking coffee at 8:00 A.M. when the delivery men showed up at my door, appliances in tow. Despite my late night latex disaster, I was going to have a lovely laundry after all.

But later that morning, driving to work, a terrible thought came to mind: what if I had died in my sleep? After all when you're single, weeks can go by before anyone notices you're not around. I could imagine my coworkers finally beginning to ask, "Has anyone seen Liz this month?" until at last the police would break into my house and find a stiff, half-naked pink woman with a starving cat perched at the foot of her bed. Gives me the willies to think about it. Ever since then, my color choices have been more subdued, a favorite being Heirloom Beige, which matches my aging skin perfectly.

Home Sweet Home

By the mid '80s, I was steeped in antiques (a fancy name for used furniture) and had hit my stride in interior design. You'll find *Country Living* stacked high in my magazine basket, quilts of every size and pattern hanging on the walls, and bargain "finds" from many a Saturday scavenger hunt. The sign I saw on the lawn outside a country collectibles store says it all: "Gifts and Goodies: Prepare to Shop."

When we moved to this, our *last* house, I finally tossed the curtain fabric from two houses ago. Now, more than ever, I love decorating my home because I get to go *shopping* to do it. Unlike our super seamstress in Proverbs 31, you and I don't have to make everything homemade . . . we just need to make it home.

20

Queen-Size Couture

Her clothing is fine linen and purple.
Proverbs 31:22b NKJV

*I*t was neither fine linen nor purple, but it was a lovely dress, one of my favorites for traveling. The first of four hours on the 727 had just begun as I settled into my coach seat, shoes off, glasses on, intent on tackling some long-neglected paperwork.

Everything was going smoothly until I got an itch in the center of my back. I tried first one hand, then the other, but couldn't quite reach that one place that was itching more with every second. Finally, I put the cap back on my felt-tip pen and poked it down the back of my dress, maneuvering it to the exact spot. I began to scratch . . . ahhh! The relief was immediate. That is, until the top of the pen came off in my hand, and the business half dropped down my back. Visions of the damage a black felt-tip pen could do to the back of an ivory dress began swimming before my eyes. The pen had stopped abruptly at the seat belt, so I leaned forward to point the dangerous end toward my back and away from my dress.

Now what? Ask the man next to me to unzip my dress and retrieve my pen? Hardly. Leave it there for another three hours? Not likely. There was no option but to stand up and try to get it out. I gingerly unbuckled the seat belt, slid forward and stood up, remaining bent over as I stepped into the aisle. A flight attendant who was witnessing all this hurried toward me.

"Miss, are you ill? The seat belt sign is still lit, and you really must be seated." All eyes were fixed on me as I straightened up, gulped and wiggled my hips. Plop! The errant black pen dropped through my dress and onto the carpet, to the astonishment of the flight attendant and two dozen nearby passengers.

I couldn't resist playing to such a captive audience. "Say!" I exclaimed, bending over to pick up the pen. "I've been looking for this for weeks!"

Perfectly Fitting

Although our Proverbs 31 woman didn't wear ivory with an occasional black splotch, she did wear purple, the color of royalty, fit for a queen. Her material was linen, the fabric of the priests, used in the temple. In other words, the "ideal woman" dresses well (hooray!) but sews it all herself (boo!).

If time permitted and I had more talent, I, too, would be sewing my own clothes. Not only out of economic necessity, but also because it's the one way to assure a perfect fit—very important for those of us with abundant bodies—as well as better quality fabric at a better price and seams that hold together for more than one trip through the wash cycle.

Instead, I shop at those stores with clothes especially designed with big, beautiful women in mind. I'm grateful for the pretty clothes, but the names are sometimes a bit much. In North Carolina, I stumbled on a store called, "The Stout Hut." Can you imagine floating into a gathering where you might want to dress to impress and admitting your queenly attire of "fine linen and purple" came from The Stout Hut?

As my last book assured each of us, *One Size Fits All* truly is a fable. Tammie from Ohio spotted this sign at her local dry cleaners: "Some stretch pants don't have a choice." Amen. Everyone's favorite funny lady, Erma Bombeck, nicely summed up the pantyhose needs of the full-figured woman: "We're looking for some nice firm sausage casings that sack up the legs and cut our losses around the waist area."[1]

I take great solace in the fact that according to 1 Corinthians, when we get to heaven, we get a new body (I've checked and it's a size 6). More good news can be found in Matthew, where we learn that "many who are first will be last, and the last first" (19:30 NKJV). Which means if you wear a 6 now . . . you'll be wearing a 24 for eternity.

No wonder we love to sing, "When we all get to heaven, what a day of rejoicing that will be"!!

A "Come As You Are" Party

It's worth noting that nowhere in this Proverbs 31 passage do we learn what an excellent woman might look like. She is not called "fair of face" or "lovely of form" or any such biblical language. No mention of her dress size either. Clothing color, yes. Fabric, sure. But size, no. Interesting.

My sweet Bill assures me he has always found my "face and form" to be attractive, even without makeup or a fancy hairdo. But when it comes to clothes, he loves it when I'm all spiffed up. "How do you want me to dress around the house, though?" I asked one day, a bit huffy. Surely he didn't expect me to wear nylons and heels at home. Shades of Donna Reed.

"No, my request is simpler than that," he said. My eyebrows shot up in anticipation. "Let's just say that pajamas are not appropriate after 10:00 A.M."

His comment has a historical basis. Since my writing and speaking office is in a cottage behind our home, going to work means walking out the back door with a cup of coffee. It also means our office dress code is, shall we say, loosely defined.

One morning I headed out to the office early, wearing my favorite p.j.s: an oversized T-shirt. I fully intended to take a shower and dress for the day, but at 7:30 I wanted to take advantage of a nice quiet place for writing.

Nine o'clock came. Pam, my office manager, came. No big deal; she'd seen me in pajamas before. Then the exterminator came. As he helped himself through the front door, I jumped behind the copier. The Minolta was no match for my bountiful body. As he made his way around the room, swishing his bug spray wand along the baseboards, I inched along the wall, eyes glued to the door. Four steps to go, then freedom. As I reached for the handle, he drawled, "Ma'am, I'm just as embarrassed as you are."

Okay, Bill, you win. No more pajamas after breakfast.

All Sown Up

But what about *your* husband? Does he have any particular requests concerning appearance or attire? Since our Proverbs passage didn't feature much along those lines, I didn't include questions on such topics in the survey. Even so, a few women mentioned adjustments to their appearance when asked what their husbands might appreciate most. Betty said, "My husband would be so proud of me if I would let my fingernails grow." Ann was sure he'd be happy if she "lost weight and grew longer hair." "Shaved my legs every day!" said Julee from Kansas.

I, for one, am thrilled that our Proverbs woman was beautifully adorned and busy doing important things but was apparently not caught up with that which does not last—earthly beauty—in order to focus on that which is eternal—heavenly character. She was not only sewing fabric, she was sowing seeds, seeds of righteousness that would bear fruit for generations, even our own.

21

Breadmaker or Breadwinner?

Her husband is known in the gates, /
When he sits among the elders of the
land.

Proverbs 31:23 NKJV

Brenda and her husband Roy have a most unusual
sentence at the top of their checks: "This Money Is
Made from Mugging Bugs." Turns out, Roy has his
own exterminating business. Their son hopes to carry on the
eighteen-year tradition, but Brenda wants to know when the
time comes, "Will there be bugs in heaven?" We hope not, but
the rest of your family is welcome. Meanwhile, you can be sure
when she cashes a check in that town, everybody "in the gates"
knows what her husband does for a living.

This verse from Proverbs might bristle the neck hairs of some
of us. "Why isn't *she* known in the gates?" we might ask. "Why is
she always in the home, and her *husband* goes where the action is,
where the business of government and society are conducted?"

No need to get our pantyhose in a knot. The Proverbs woman
will indeed be "known in the gates" for her good deeds by the
time we hit verse 31. The fact that her husband is respected
there, too, is just another feather in her cap. They make a
dynamite team, just like Brenda and Roy.

Bill and I have an interesting situation in that I left my full-time job at WHAS-AM in 1987 and he started at WHAS-TV two years later, in 1989. Although they are now owned by two different companies, our radio and TV stations were in the same building and shared several staff members. When I went to his first Christmas party, I was taken aback that so few people remembered me, but everybody knew Bill, of course. I was introduced again and again as "Bill's wife." Now, *he* was "known in the gates," and I wasn't. Bah, humbug! The evening turned out to be a fairly severe ego squash for me.

It was also a reminder that the world does not ascribe much value to the stay-at-home mother. People said things like, "Didn't you used to be Liz Curtis?" or the old standby, "What do you do all day?" My customary response was to look at them with my head held high and say, "I'm molding, shaping, and influencing the next generation. What do *you* do all day?"

Psychologist Dr. Layne Longfellow observes that in our society, historically, "we have assigned love to women and work to men." Of course, today we have women who love working and men who are working at being more loving. Dr. Longfellow suggests, "We have to create permission for women to find their own individual balance between work and love, intimacy and competency."[1] My intent here has been to affirm both the stay-at-home mother and the mother who works outside the home. If a woman is in tune with her God and her partner, then her choices about gates or no gates is in good hands.

"Iron John" or the Tin Man?

Since this verse focuses on what the husband of the ideal wife is about, suppose we train our camera on the men for a chapter or so and see how they measure up to her standards, as well as ours.

Breathes there a man on this planet worthy of being called perfect? Joanne admits that "even though he is not perfect, my husband is perfect for me!" Vivian cautions, "There are no perfect husbands, only men who make the most of positives in their mates and ignore the negatives." From Anita come these words of wisdom: "The older I get, the more I accept that there is no perfect husband, and that has helped our relationship."

 ### Her husband is known in the gates, / When he sits among the elders of the land.

We had all sorts of stereotypes for describing the "perfect wife"—Donna Reed, June Cleaver, Betty Crocker, Mae West—but no names popped up in our descriptions for the husband. We didn't profess a desire to be married to John Wayne, Rhett Butler, the Galloping Gourmet, or Fred Flintstone. Not even Mel Gibson's name came up as an example of Mr. Perfect (though now that we've mentioned it . . .).

What we *did* find appealing is a man who "loves unconditionally, can handle 'mood swings,' and is involved with the children," said Rebecca. Someone who is "always there for you, even when you let the fuel injected car run out of gas (that's a bad thing to do)," wrote Linda from Arkansas. Sheri thinks "perfect" would be a man who "wouldn't grumble because things are out of place and the kids are whining."

Susan from Alabama remembers how helpful her husband was late one night:

When my son was teething, he woke up several times crying, and my husband finally volunteered to get up and care for him. As he got out of bed he asked me where the teething ointment was. "In the diaper bag," I told him. He never turned the light on, just reached in the bag, got out a tube and squeezed it, and smeared it on the baby's gums.

My husband thought it felt funny—"too sticky"—so he turned on the light and discovered he had coated the baby's gums with diaper rash ointment! Here the two of them came, running into our bedroom, my baby's mouth covered with white stuff as he licked his lips! We called the poison center, and they assured us that there wasn't enough zinc in the ointment to harm the baby. They also wanted to know if it helped his teething pain. It must have—he slept the rest of the night!

I think she means the baby. I'm not sure about the husband.

I like Bea from North Dakota's wish list for a man: "Partial hearing loss. Suggests eating out often." A man who *fixes* what needs fixing!" appeals to Sonya. Finally, there's Sherri from West Virginia and her version of the ideal sweetie: "Caring, good listener, loving, respectful, honest, plus can kill *all* types of 'creepy-crawlies'"!

In response to this "describe the perfect husband" question, the legal department of a large company in Charlotte faxed to me a list of "Seminars for Men" that, ostensibly, female staff members would be offering to the men in their company:

Course #104: "How to Fill the Ice Tray"
(I wonder if they'd have a correspondence course for Bill.)

Course #123: "The Remote Control—Overcoming Your Dependency"
(I just hide it!)

Course #130: "Real Men Ask for Directions"
(Helpful women take maps.)

The sign-up sheet reminded interested parties that "class size will be limited to ten as course material may prove difficult."

Now this kind of spoof is funny, no doubt about it. When I showed the list to Bill, he laughed as he read it but then handed it back to me and said, "If the men in our office circulated a similar list of seminars for women, the females would raise the roof." Of course, he's right. Hm-m-m.

All Hail the Working Father

Patty from Indiana believes she married the perfect husband—"or at least he's as close as men come!" She wrote, "From the time I went back to work following the birth of our son six years ago, my husband has been a full-time working dad. Right from the start he took our son with him on visits to hospitals and shut-ins (he's a minister). My son learned social skills that most children his age never get the opportunity to learn."

Not only does this wonder man help with childcare, but "his roasts and chickens are great! He also sometimes cleans and runs the vacuum. Since we've been married, we've tried to operate our household under the idea of whoever has the most time pitches in to do what needs [to be] done."

For my money, Patty and her husband have the best kind of contemporary marriage: a team. She obviously adores him, he is committed to her, and they both love their son. Undoubtedly, all three of them are "known in the gates" as a fine example of family.

22
Delivereth Us from Girdles

She makes linen garments and sells
them, / And supplies sashes for the
merchants.

Proverbs 31:24 NKJV

The good old King James translation says she "delivereth girdles unto the merchant." Great idea. Let the merchants wear them. I was delivered from those instruments of torture back in 1968 with the advent of pantyhose. A blessing, I think.

Our Proverbs role model chose the best of both worlds: working at home, then delivering her girdles—uh, sashes or belts—to the gates for the merchants to sell. Very clever woman, this. In the current vernacular, we would say she had a cottage industry.

Brenda Hunter, author of *Where Have All the Mothers Gone?* said, "Women who use their gifts or hobbies to create their own businesses are among the most satisfied working mothers I know."[1] Lots of us are seeking that satisfaction these days. According to LINK Resources, "The number of self-employed women working full time at home tripled between 1985 and 1991, from 378,000 to 1.1 million."[2] *Tripled!* That's more than a trend, that's an avalanche.

Mind Your Own Business

The survey question that produced some of the most interesting results was this one: "If money were not at all a consideration, I would . . ." (circle one)

Quit working

Find a more satisfying job

Keep the same job

Start my own business

One option I did not offer, and should have, was "Go back to school," but several wrote that one in anyway.

Here's what we chose: Thirty percent wanted to quit working; of those, half were mothers with children, who preferred to be home with their kids. Forty percent were happy to keep their current job, either from a high degree of enjoyment or a sense of job security. And, 9 percent were ready for greener pastures and would seek more satisfying work.

That left a full 21 percent of us who would, if money were available, start our own businesses. Add to that the dozens of women who filled out the survey and already owned their own businesses, and that's an impressive number! And what if some of the 30 percent, rather than quit work altogether, could come up with a creative way to earn money at home? And what if those looking for more satisfaction decided they would find it by working for themselves? That would add up to more than 60 percent of us! The potential for women working at home is viable, exciting, and certainly the direction many of us are headed for in the twenty-first century.

What home businesses come to mind? In her wonderful collection of advice called *The Mommy Book,* Karen Hull suggests several: home typing (or data entry), proofreading, music lessons, dressmaking and alterations, crafts, home baby-sitting, catering.[3] These are what we might call the traditional home-based businesses for women, and they are still very legitimate pursuits. After all, our Proverbs 31 woman is qualified to do *all* of them—though not at the same time, of course.

On the surveys, we found that women dreamed of being: an interior designer, a consultant, an artist, a travel writer, a horse breeder and trainer, and "a party planner for working moms." (Where do I sign up for *her* services?)

Two different women in Texas expressed a desire to own their own craft stores and fill them with their creations. I'm tempted to put them together and watch what might happen if their mutual dream took shape! Another woman wanted to run a clothing store, and Gloria dreamed of owning "a wildly successful wedding catering business." My favorite answer was the woman who circled "Start my own business," then listed her dream occupation as "astronaut." Boy, the start-up costs on *that* one would be . . . astronomical!

First, the Bad News

For those women and thousands more among us who have seriously thought about working from home, let me gently dispel three myths about the advantages of owning a home business:

1. Flexible Hours

When someone asks me where I work and I say, "I have a speaking business with an office behind my house," their immediate reaction is, "It must be so nice to make your own hours!" I sure do . . . *all* of them. A home-based business takes quite a while to establish, so in the first twelve to thirty-six months, you are working every chance you get. When the kids nap, Mom works. At school? Mom works. Asleep at night? Mom works. Although you won't need to punch a time clock, it might be worthwhile to jot down your hours each day to get a feel of how much this "little business" requires of your life. Most self-employed women I know put in fifty to seventy hours a week and don't sleep much.

2. Convenience with No Commuting

The phrase "run your business out of your home" can

easily be reversed to, "your business runs you out of *your* home!" What began in the back corner of our back bedroom soon engulfed the room so completely we had to take the bed out and put in a second desk and storage shelves. Soon, all my paper supplies—cards, letterhead, envelopes, brochures, articles, and so on—began flowing out of the bedroom-turned-office and into the living room. At first, the boxes were just going to be there for a few days, and a month later, three more were stacked on top. We tried moving the boxes to an upstairs closet . . . *not* good. The plaster ceiling in our dining room collapsed under the weight of all that paper! Suffice to say, a business at home is handy but hard to contain.

3. Big Bucks

It *is* nice to know that whatever money you bring in is all yours. Well, almost all yours. The IRS will take a big chunk, especially with that nice self-employment tax on top of paying all your other taxes yourself. Plus there are no benefits, such as health or life insurance, unless you buy them. Then, add in office supplies, printing, marketing, advertising, long-distance phone calls—the list goes on and on, depending on the business. The more it grows, the more it costs to maintain. Nothing will mess up your profit margin like success! Many of our "one woman shows" grew such that we had to hire an employee or two, which for many of us turned out to be our single greatest business expense. Somewhere on that spreadsheet is a perfect balance between the top line—gross—and the bottom line—net. ʼnfortunately, many small businesses struggle to find that optimum spot between profit and loss.

Now, the Good News

If I've discouraged you from starting your own business, that's good! It is not for everyone and should not be entered into lightly.

But there are some distinct benefits that don't carry to the bottom line but do connect nicely to the heart line. Working in the back bedroom when my children were little, I would play footsie with Matthew as he crawled about on a quilt at my feet. He was a very happy baby and stayed that way as long as Mother was in view. Especially in the first year, children really do sleep a lot, so finding time to make phone calls and type letters was not difficult.

After Lillian came along twenty months later, things got noisier, and clients would occasionally ask, "Who is making all that racket in the background?"

I would reply cooly, "Senior management."

When he was old enough to reach the keys, I taught Matthew how to push the buttons on the calculator to make the place sound more like a busy office and less like a busy nursery. The children always went with me on errand runs, to the post office or the printer, and solved the one problem that often plagues a sole proprietor: isolation and loneliness.

She makes linen garments and sells them, / And supplies sashes for the merchants.

As they are growing, the kids are able to help me with some of the busy work that goes along with any small business: putting stamps on envelopes, attaching mailing labels, putting packing peanuts in boxes, and so forth. We make it a game (which means it takes twice as long), but they *are* the reason I wanted to work out of my home in the first place!

When you have your own business in your home, you have a hard time explaining what you do for Career Day at school. Telling five-year-olds that you're a speaker draws a Big Blank, so I started drawing them into the discussion by asking, "What are *you* going to do when you grow up?" One angelic-faced child turned very pink and stammered, "I'm not going to do *anything* until I get married!" This child has been well trained.

If the survey results are representative, our husbands would love to see us enjoy career success, too, especially if it greatly increases the family's bottom line. Denise said her husband would be so proud of her if she "accomplished a major task, like write a book." As long as he understands that you'll probably never get rich that way, go for it! Judy thought her hubby would be happy if she "made $100,000 a year or more." Right. Finally, Brenda from Hawaii just knew her husband would be pleased if she were "chief money earner and sex kitten." (The only way she could have the energy to be both is if she were a money earner *as* a sex kitten, and that's probably out!)

Whether we make those girdles for the merchants at home or on a job site, some of us have found our husbands may enjoy the extra income but resent our commitment of time and energy to the task, "particularly when they feel their wives aren't giving them the kind of attention they want," noted author Bebe Campbell. She also discovered many instances when women who carefully selected a mate who promised to aid and support them in their professional goals "were angry because their husbands withdrew the support just when they needed it most."[4] It's especially important when home is our place of work that our families be included in the decision making. I've always said that talking quietly now prevents talking loudly later. Bill's goal for our marriage-family-work combo is to land somewhere between Ozzie and Harriet and separate vacations.

Encouragement, Please!

The most important ingredient for success when working at home is to have a network of friends to encourage you, pitch in when needed, and spread the word. Precious is the friend who understands that this *is* a real job—with hours, commitments, and deadlines—yet knows that your family responsibilities come first, and supports your attempts to combine the two.

Debbie from Ohio included a plea for encouragement about going back to work. "I know I can do it," she wrote. "I know my family will survive. It's just taking the plunge that is difficult." No question, it will require some days (weeks? months?) of adjustment, but your family may thrive, not just survive.

What we need most from one another as women is support and positive reinforcement for our businesses, our choices, and our balancing acts. I spoke at a church one Sunday evening, with the children and Bill seated in the front pew. I was so proud of them: they didn't make any faces at me, and even Bill laughed at stories he'd heard a dozen times. When I went to the back of the church at the close of the program, a dear woman came up to me, took my hand, and looked me in the eye. I was certain she was going to join the chorus of, "I thoroughly enjoyed your message," or (oh dear!), "I've never heard a woman speaker before. What did you say your name was again, honey?"

But here's what she said: "Liz, I watched you with your children this evening. You must be a pretty special mom."

Thank you, thank you, thank you. As much as we all enjoy praise for our work, most of us could really use some encouragement in those less visible arenas. Mark Twain said, "I can live for two months on a good compliment." Better than that. So far, I've lived on her kind words for four years!

On the Road with Mom

I found lots of words to encourage us in a nifty book by Katherine Wyse Goldman called *My Mother Worked and I Turned Out Okay*. It's the kind of book you read and say, "Boy, I wish I'd written that!" Since she did, and I didn't, here are two of her brilliant observations:

• Children who know what their mothers do all day at work are more inclined to tell their mothers what they do all day at school.

- Working mothers are masters at including the kids and making everybody think it was a good idea.[5]

I especially love to include the kids when we travel. When I spoke in Montana, Alaska, Michigan, Ohio, and Missouri, the whole family went. *Big* fun. When I spoke in Orlando, five-year-old Matthew went along, so when the speech was over we could visit—where else?—Disney World.

Lillian was the star attraction on a speaking jaunt to Pennsylvania, where various relatives amused her while I spoke and my mother-in-law came along to be of service. I still remember changing Lillian's diaper during our tour of the Lancaster County countryside. We were way out in the middle of nowhere, and there wasn't a dumpster in sight. The only containers to be found were rural mailboxes. Just for a second, we considered slipping our little "bomb" in one of them, putting the flag up, and hitting the gas! You'll be relieved to know we did no such thing.

Sometimes I do have to travel alone, but those trips are generally twenty-four hours long, and I'm back home before too much damage is done to the house. Although the travel is the most challenging part of my business, it's also my best source of stories. Staying at a hotel in Mason City, Iowa, I called down to the front desk and asked them to kindly send up an iron and an ironing board, which they dutifully did. Attached to this big ironing board was a little tag to remind me it belonged to the Sheraton. But, on the flip side of the tag it said: "If carried away inadvertently, drop in any mailbox."

In all my years of staying in hotels, I have never found myself in the lobby saying, "Oh, my word, there's an ironing board in my purse!" Nor have I ever seen a woman trying to stuff one in a mailbox. A diaper maybe, but never an ironing board.

The truth is, I don't work at home. I *play* at home and get paid for it—which should be the goal of all our labors, wherever and however they take place. Katharine Graham said it perfectly: "To love what you do and feel that it matters . . . how could anything be more fun?"

23
Dressed for Success

Strength and honor are her clothing.
Proverbs 31:25 NKJV

Boy, could this woman dress! Not just in linen like the priests, not just in purple like royalty, not just in her own fabulous handmade creations, but she wore strength like a shield. In the Hebrew, the word means "mighty fortress" and "powerful stronghold." Sounds like the hymn that Luther wrote: "A mighty fortress is our God."

And she was clothed in honor, meaning "dignity, splendor, majesty, and beauty," from head to toe. The truth is, when you are attired in such timeless virtues and that's what people see first, you really are dressed for success.

What makes her godly attire especially attractive is the combination: strength *and* honor. We've all known women who were strong, but not very honorable. Our television screens are filled with them. And there are women who are honorable, but frankly, not very strong. The first setback or the first perceived threat, and they fold up like a card table.

The kind of women most of us long to be are both strong and honorable, clothed with the kind of power that comes from on high, certain of our value in God's eyes, definite in our calling, and moving forward with complete assurance. Francis De Sales said, "Nothing is so strong as gentleness, nothing so gentle as real strength."

Strong, Honorable . . . and a Little Nervous

Gale from Kentucky needed all the strength and dignity she could muster to get her through this experience. When her son was fourteen, he wanted to have some friends over to "camp out" behind the barn.

As the planning and telephone calls began, I had the feeling he had something else up his sleeve. Finally he told me some girls might come by but only for a little while. "Okay," I said, trying to be a cool mom while knowing I was going to watch them like a hawk!

The evening came and so did the guys. We visited with them for a while and asked where the girls were. Disappointed faces and shrugged shoulders told us the guys had been stood up. I must say, I was relieved, and my husband and I went on to bed.

Around 11:00, I heard the gravel in the driveway. I couldn't believe it! The girls had arrived. What should I do? I didn't want to make a scene, so I decided to watch from the upstairs bedroom window. The kids stood around and talked, and after about ten minutes, the car pulled out. Good!

The next morning, I went out to see if everything was cleaned up, and other than a few plastic cups, they'd done a nice job. I bent over to pick up a napkin and saw what I had hoped I'd never see. There it was, a small square package with a round indentation in the center. The edges were torn back. No doubt about it—there was a condom in my yard!

A million thoughts crashed through my mind: "Maybe it was longer than ten minutes? Maybe one of the girls had stayed behind? What would I say to my son? How should I handle this?"

All this between seeing the package and bending down to pick it up. Then I turned it over to read the label: "Alka Seltzer." Can you believe it?! I almost ended up in the coronary unit because some kid had an upset stomach!

Yes, we can believe it.

"Strong Enough for a Man, Gentle Enough for a Woman"

Notice that our Proverbs woman is not dressed for battle. In the '70s and '80s women wore business attire like a suit of armor as we headed out to slay dragons in the business world. "I can dress like, think like, and work like a man," our clothing said. "I can fit into Corporate America." Reminds me of an old pack of stick-'em notes I found in the deep recesses of my desk, which showed "The Career Woman's checklist for success: look like a lady, act like a man, work like a dog." That was "strength" to us not long ago.

Now wisdom and balance are creeping back in, and we are finding out what it really means to "dress for success." As the Amplified version says, "Strength and dignity are her clothing and her position is strong and secure."

Since I am a woman who is, shall we say, strong-willed, forthright, not afraid to state her mind, aggressive, powerful, and other words folks have used over the years that are *not* appropriate to print, I have always questioned how to use my strong personality in a dignified way. Teresa from Kansas stated it exactly: "My assertiveness sometimes sounds aggressive."

For Teresa and me, and maybe you, Peter Guber advised, "The trick is to use the least amount of power to create the maximum amount of change. Someone who has elegance can apply power selectively like a laser," and do so "carefully, almost unobtrusively, so that you don't feel you're being overpowered. You feel like you're being motivated."[1]

Another mark of dignity is our ability to use strength for the good of others, and not simply for our personal advancement. Kate Halverson once said, "If you are all wrapped up in yourself, you are overdressed."[2]

Dressed for All Eternity

If, as the original Hebrew words suggest, this woman's strength and dignity are grounded in her spirituality, it might be worth looking into who our spiritual role models might be.

On the surveys, many left the question, "Who is your spiritual role model?" blank. Others wrote: "unsure," "never gave it much thought—I really don't know," "I don't have a spiritual role model," "?? I guess I don't have or want one," "it's strange, I've never thought about this," and "big vacuum here—I've lost it."

I always appreciate the honesty of someone willing to respond to such a personal question at all. Until a dozen years ago, I would've answered with a big question mark myself. For many of us, when we moved into our thirties, into marriage, or into motherhood, the questions those new roles raised triggered a desire within us to explore the spiritual side of ourselves again, or perhaps for the first time.

Strength and honor are her clothing.

Our role models in the area of spirituality are both wide and deep. More than one hundred of us specifically wrote down "God." Nancy looks up to "the Lord—his understanding, his strength, everything." Doris wrote, "Jesus—his ability to love and forgive." Molly chose, "God the Father—he has never given me bad advice."

Others of us listed role models with flesh on them, such as Sandy who admires her pastor whose "life is glowing with God's light and love." Anita mentioned "a Sunday school teacher of years ago," and Joan described a woman whom I also greatly admire, "Mother Teresa . . . she is so caring and giving."

Gayle honored "St. Jude (for lost causes) because that's almost the state of our house!" Cara turned to friends with fur on them for spiritual nurturing, listing "animals in general and young children." Indeed, their innocence and closeness to their Creator point us in the right direction.

Then, there's Mary Anne who included among her spiritual role models, "Angels—for reassurance." Besides, everyone knows that angels wear the most heavenly wardrobe around!

24
A Laugh a Day Puts Wrinkles in the Right Places

~~~

She smiles at the future.

Proverbs 31:25b NASB

Any woman who can, as the Hebrew declares, "smile, laugh, make merry, celebrate, rejoice, and have no fear" about the future is my kind of role model. She didn't just smile, she snorted. She didn't just giggle, she guffawed. She didn't just snicker, she roared. What a woman! As Bonnie Altenhein wrote in *How Angels Get Their Wings,* "An angel adopts grinning as a second language."[1]

My role models growing up were all funny women. First, I loved Lucy. And Ethel. Then, I longed to be Carol Burnett and was jealous for years that Vicki Lawrence got to be on her show and I didn't. Phyllis Diller, who said, "A smile is a curve that sets everything straight," was always a favorite, talking about her husband, Fang. Lily Tomlin is brilliant and off-beat, and Gilda Radner was a sprite who still twinkles in our hearts.

The funniest women to me are the ones who initiate humor, rather than follow after it or play the straight person: that is to say, Bea Arthur as Maude, rather than Jean Stapleton as Edith Bunker (though she is as fine a comic actress as they come!). It takes a certain kind of woman to shake off the "women can't tell jokes" stereotype and venture out on her own into the humor limelight.

Society values a sense of humor, consistently ranking it in the top five desirable attributes for an employee or a spouse. Among the Navajo Indians there is a tradition known as "The First Laugh Ceremony." The friend or family member who witnesses the baby's first laugh is given the privilege of throwing a celebration in honor of the occasion, considered to mark the child's entrance into society.[2]

Our sense of humor may assert itself at a young age but may not always be applauded. Bette Midler once said, "If only I'd known that one day my differentness would be an asset, then my earlier life would have been much easier."[3] So true! Yet, if I were "normal," I wouldn't be a humorist. Finding humor requires the ability to see life through glasses that aren't so much rose-colored as they are bifocals; they throw us off balance and so provide another view of things.

Take the advertisement I found for Johnson's Swabs in a woman's magazine. The copy read: "Johnson's Swabs now come in beautiful decorator canisters. . . . One for every room of the house." Immediately, my curiosity was aroused; I must have missed this in home ec. Are we supposed to have swabs in every room? Tissues, maybe, but *swabs?* I suppose you could choose a decorator canister to match your dining room set, just in case your guests want to clean their ears before dinner.

I like George Burns's philosophy: "If I get big laughs, I'm a comedian. I get little laughs, I'm a humorist. If I get no laughs, I'm a singer." Believe me, when I perform, I have a song ready, just in case!

Too Busy to Laugh Is Too Busy

Of course, to be like our Proverbs woman and smile at the days to come, we need to do more chuckling in the present. Our modern sisters are not doing nearly enough merry-making, I can tell you that. When I encourage women to laugh more, they tell me in tight-lipped, terse tones, "I'm too busy to laugh. I don't have time to rent a funny video, and even if I did, I don't have time to watch it. I don't have time to buy a funny book, and even if I did, I don't have time to read it. I just don't have time for foolishness!"

That's us, all right. Poor dears, we are missing the Big Picture, which is that all work and no play makes Jill not only a dull girl, but also a sick one. Laughter is good for our hearts, souls, and minds. It costs virtually nothing, yet its therapeutic effect tops many an expensive medicine.

In theory, we know what we need: "more laughter, less mail!" "more fun, less worrying"; "more chocolate, fewer complications"; and my favorite, from Laura in Ohio, "more private bathroom time and less saturated fat!"

Laughing is the one time we express our true selves, our true nature. There is *no* such thing as "image laughing." You can learn how to walk, stand, sit, eat properly, but when you laugh, you lay all pretense aside and just let go. That's why laughing is so good for you. Anyway, Fred Allen says, "It's bad to suppress laughter. It goes right back down and spreads to your hips."

We know we need to lighten up: "After a bad day at work, a poopy diaper, and six trips for a glass of water at bedtime . . . I need a laugh!" wrote Pam. Carol said, "Make me laugh at things we sometimes take too seriously—like housework." Oh, that's always a laugh at our house. And, concerning this book, Marsha from New Mexico wanted to hear about "both the fun and the *not* so fun aspects of life" as well as how we can "survive it all with humor." The truth is, we can't survive *without* humor.

Children Have Funny Bones Too

Few things make us smile more than children and the things they say. Sandra from Mississippi stifled a laugh when they brought home a cocker spaniel puppy and their youngest asked if that meant it would bark in Spanish. On another occasion, when their car was just turning over 50,000 miles, she was showing her boys where to look on the dash, to which the youngest said, "We'll have to get gas soon, huh, Mom?"

Molly from North Dakota remembered the evening her six-year-old came in from playing with a friend. He was "talking very fast, his eyes like saucers. 'Mom, Mom, Joshua was telling me all about the boogey monster, and I got the willies!'" She asked him, "What are the willies, Daniel?" to which he replied, "You know, when you get willy scared and willy nervous!"

Once those little ones grow up, not everything they say is so cute and funny. One woman admitted, "I hope the Lord comes back before my son turns thirteen!" Meanwhile, if we have husbands, we can count on their sense of humor remaining childlike—or is that juvenile?—forever. Comedian Jay Leno admitted, "All men laugh at the Three Stooges, and all women think they are dumb. When Moe hits Larry with a shovel, the guy cracks up; the woman will get up, mutter 'Stupid!' and turn the set off. When was the last time you saw two women go, 'Nyuk, Nyuk, Nyuk'?"[4]

My Husband, the Humorist

Come to think of it, Bill's sense of humor is very different from mine. His is a dry wit, quiet and clever. Mine is all bold and physical and pratfalls and big grins. As in all things, we are very different when it comes to what makes us laugh and how we make others laugh.

To this day, I'm not sure whether Bill meant this to be funny or not. For my first Mother's Day, instead of getting something sweet for the nursery or something romantic, he got me a fishing license.

This was not on my wish list for Mother's Day, but it was on *his* list for Father's Day. When he checked into it, he found out that Kentucky sells a husband-and-wife fishing license. It's a little cheaper that way, and Bill, remember, is tight. The license must show the exact height and weight for both spouses, so Bill filled out my half for me. He told those nice people in Frankfort that I am 5'9" (correct), 132 pounds (not correct). Not even close. Even taking a stab-in-the-dark guess, you would come up with a higher number. A much higher number.

So, I'm looking in his eyes for a clue. Is he kidding, or is he serious? He's so analytical, maybe he thought to himself: "I wear a size 44 suit, and Liz wears a size 22 dress. Maybe she's about half my size?"

Finally, the gleam in his eye suggested that I had been had.

"You turkey!" I said with a wink. "What am I going to say when the Fish and Game Commissioner stops us and wants to see our license? 'Sorry, sir, I stopped at Hardee's!'?"

Holy Humor

I have a soft place in my heart for the good old days of television: of watching Carol Burnett transform herself into a washer woman, of watching Jack Benny fold his arms just so, of hearing Red Skelton, a man who once said, "If I can make people smile, then I have served my purpose for God," end his show by whispering, "God bless." We can still watch Dick Van Dyke fall over the ottoman on late night reruns, but I miss the variety shows, the live television comedy hours, even the early years of *Saturday Night Live*.

Of course, as Griff Niblak in the *Indianapolis News* said, "If you're yearning for the good old days, just turn off the air conditioning." Maybe not. Maybe we need to be like our proverbial sister and smile, not at the past, but at the future. One commentator wrote, "She has full confidence in her ability and resources to meet the challenges of the future. Perhaps, this is her most enviable characteristic."[5]

Reinhold Niebuhr, best known for penning the Serenity Prayer, also wrote: "Humor is a prelude to faith, and laughter is the beginning of prayer." For those who love God, laughter isn't optional, it's scriptural. As we all love to repeat, "A merry heart doeth good like a medicine" (Prov. 17:22 KJV). As a woman who believes in the power of faith *and* humor, I am heaven-bent to bring more laughter into our lives.

Joy shows up in the Bible more than two hundred times, but I wish there were more in there about laughter. After all, we know "Jesus wept" (John 11:35 NKJV). Why not another nice short verse to assure us, "Jesus laughed"? Cal Samra, founder of the Fellowship of Merry Christians, of which I'm proud to be a member, offers valid proof that Jesus did indeed laugh. "We know that Jesus loved children, who laugh frequently and spontaneously." Samra rightly suggests that he also laughed "at the bumblings of his all-too-human disciples, who were missing the point and messing things up."[6]

I wonder if the big blast of sound we call laughter today might not have been what the psalmist had in mind when he wrote, "Shout joyfully to the LORD, all the earth" (Ps. 98:4 NKJV). After all, they had other words for singing. And if two million Israelites stood around shouting "Hooray for God!" at the top of their lungs, somebody had to start laughing sooner or later.

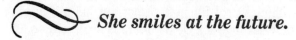 *She smiles at the future.*

We all see and hear things each day that make us shout joyfully. For her job as an educational consultant, Stacy from Kansas does some home visits with families. "I asked one lady for directions, and she promptly replied, 'I live in the third house on the passenger side of the street.'" Oh, that's helpful.

Or there was the sign I saw in the window of a music store: "Used Organs for Sale." Are we talking spleens and kidneys in the piano benches, or what?

Another favorite sign appeared on the outskirts of a small town with one fast food restaurant—not McDonald's. This was "Skeeter's: Home of the Big Biscuit." The big hand-lettered sign hanging out front said, with no punctuation: "Drive Thru 50 Item Salad Bar." I pictured a family of four, all leaning out of their Suburban, trying to keep the croutons from blowing off their salads. "Dad, back up, I missed the dressing!"

Driving through western Kentucky recently, I found myself on the Pennyrile Parkway, a toll road. When I came to the first exit, the Department of Transportation folks had posted a big sign: "Do Not Exit Without Exact Change."

Sure doesn't give you many choices. I'm thinking, *Why didn't they put that sign up before I got on?* People have been driving the Pennyrile for weeks, just hoping to pick up a hitchhiker with the exact change.

When the Laughter Stops

When you are the one people turn to for laughter—the life of the party, the class clown, the raconteur—people expect you to always be on, to be funny all the time. Even those of us who make people laugh for a living can't live up to that expectation. My first pastor, Bob Russell, tells the story of a man who had fallen into such a deep depression that he finally placed himself in the hands of a therapist.

"I have an unusual prescription for you," the therapist told him. "The circus is in town, and last night I saw the funniest clown there ever was. Thirty minutes of watching the Great Rinaldi, and you'll feel 100 percent better."

With tears in his eyes, the patient replied, "I am the Great Rinaldi."

I have yet to meet a humorist, a comedian, or a clown that didn't have some deep hurt at the heart of his or her humor. When we laugh at something, we are in essence saying, "I identify with that!" If someone stood up and described all their blessings, we would be disgusted. When they stand up and share all their faults and foibles, we laugh and love them for it. Rosita Perez kindly encouraged me in a letter with these words: "Whoever says laughter isn't healing just hasn't hurt enough."

Laughter does not mean you are ignoring pain, living in denial, or just not aware of the troubles around you. Solomon said, "Even in laughter the heart may ache" (Prov. 14:13 NIV). For me, laughter is how we take a much-needed break from the heartache, such that when we turn to face it again, it has by some miracle grown smaller in size and intensity, if not disappeared altogether.

An Oklahoma woman wrote, "Laughter was the prescription to help me deal with the unfaithfulness and abandonment by my husband for a woman younger than our two oldest daughters. A laugh a day—a good belly laugh—made me well."

We women need to help each other heal our hurts with laughter. That's really my mission in life, why I speak, why I write. I've watched women who were almost bent over with arthritis laugh until they forgot to hurt. "Look at this!" they call out, waving their arms in the air with glee. "No pain!"

And I've known women who've shared their deepest sorrows with me, how they've lost touch with God and with themselves, then I watch them, sitting in the audience, tears of joy streaming down their faces. "Are you laughing or crying?" I ask them.

"Yes!" they reply.

25
Open Mouth, Insert Kindness

She opens her mouth with wisdom, /
And on her tongue is the law of kindness.

Proverbs 31:26 *NKJV*

She parted her lips to smile, laugh, and make merry; now it's time for her to speak! After fifteen verses describing her glorious talents, her skillful hands and her sacrificial schedule, the woman is finally going to open her mouth and tell us what is on her mind and in her heart: wisdom and kindness, of course.

We are not surprised. Her actions have already spoken loudly on her behalf. Her husband, children, friends, neighbors, even those elders at the gate paid attention when she opened her mouth.

When Brandy from Oregon described a perfect wife, she hit the old nail on the head for this Proverbs woman: "She's patient, intuitive, patient, kind, patient, thoughtful, patient, strong, and has the patience of Job!"

A Little Whine with Dinner

Most of us, however, do not have the patience of Lot's wife, let alone that of Job. Looking over some of the things we would like to modify about ourselves, it's comforting to know that many of us share the same struggles with loose lips. With the names removed to protect the guilty, here's what we'd like to change when we open our mouths:

"Be less critical"

"Talk less"

"Communicate in a more positive and mature way"

"Do less criticizing and yelling"

"Think before I speak"

"Less whining"

"Stop yelling for no reason"

"Control my tongue"

All I can say is: "Me too!" As one who speaks for a living, I shudder to think of how many wasted words, empty phrases, and meaningless mumblings I've gone through in my career. To help me improve my skills, I've dutifully sat through numerous professional development seminars to teach me how to be a more effective speaker, when the answer was here in Proverbs 31 all along.

By example, our ancient sister provides a simple three-point, how-to presentation:

1. First, she spoke with actions, doing good deeds with great skill.

2. Therefore, her "audiences" sat up and paid attention.

3. Then, she was able to offer words of wisdom and instruction.

Mark Twain had her pegged: "Few things are harder to put up with than the annoyance of a good example!" It was because she spoke from a position of strength and firsthand knowledge that people were willing, even eager, to listen to her wisdom, steeped in kindness.

Where does wisdom come from, anyway? We get it from people we trust and admire, like parents, teachers, leaders, role models. Wisdom comes from experience too. A fact, lived out, becomes experience. An experience repeated becomes wisdom.

Good Books

I find wisdom in books too. *Jacob the Baker* by Noah ben Shea is filled with wisdom. The book of Proverbs is even called "Wisdom Literature." *Mere Christianity* by C. S. Lewis and *Practicing the Presence of God* by Brother Lawrence are books I turn to again and again because of their wisdom.

There's one problem with books. I'll read something wonderful, close it up, put it on a shelf, and not have the faintest idea where I read that great idea. Short of reading the book again, I have no way of locating it.

The solution is obvious: I am learning to write in my books—to underline, circle, make notes, do whatever I please. See, I always thought books were stamped "Fragile." No bending down the corners, no highlighting, and no writing in the margins. So much for that. When I'm through with a book now, it looks read. Dogeared pages, two and three colors of pens, scribbled words, and totally stray ideas jotted in the back cover. Mercy!

Now, not only has the book become part of me, but I've also become part of it. We have history together. When I take it off the shelf, I can see clearly the wisdom I've gained not only from the book itself, but from the days I've lived since the last time I read it.

What Children Say

Diana from Kentucky remembers when a book figured in to her daughter's costume for Career Day. "When my daughter was in fifth grade, she showed up in the kitchen one Tuesday morning dressed in her finest Sunday attire. 'Where's my Bible?' she asked. 'On the shelf in your room,' was my quick but baffled reply. 'Why?'

"She replied sweetly, 'It's Career Day, and I'm going as a mistress.' Being a wise mother, I knew that if she truly was going to school as a 'mistress,' she most certainly needed that Bible. 'Do you know what a mistress is?' I inquired. 'Of course I do!' she stormed. 'It's a female minister!'"

Our children expect us to be full of wisdom and know everything. Penny from Alaska's four-year-old once announced, "Mom, God made us!"

She was thrilled and said "That's right, son! God made us."

Then he asked, "But, how do they put heads on?"

Their seven-year-old daughter, equally interested in spiritual things, asked her father, "Will everybody who goes to church go to heaven? You know, like the Jehovah's Witnesses and the Ft. Lauderdale Saints?"

> *She opens her mouth with wisdom, / And on her tongue is the law of kindness.*

Crystell from Oklahoma remembers when her four-year-old son discovered "toe jam," that mysterious lint that hides between our toes. She told him, "That's why it's so important that you take a bath every night," to which he replied, "How come? It will just come back again."

Jessica, also four, was obviously very frustrated when her mother told her, "Honey, your shoes are on the wrong feet." The child replied with an exasperated sigh, "But, Mommeeee, they're the only feet I have!"

What Children Shouldn't Hear

Our children probably hear more of our words than anyone else. In the first two years, they are listening to vowels and consonants and words, so they can imitate us and say something we'll recognize: "Ma-ma!" Such music to our ears. In the pre-school years, they're listening for grammar and usage and sentence construction, to make their needs known more clearly. Once in school, language becomes a means of getting an "A" with a star on your paper, or getting a "D" with a lecture. Words, wisdom, and kindness are what a child's life is all about.

Which is why I am so disappointed in myself when I think of how often I open my mouth to criticize, gossip, make a catty remark, praise myself, speak in anger, or offer some unsupportive comment.

It was Ben Franklin who said, "Anger is never without reason, but seldom with a good one." For no valid reason whatsoever, many people live on the edge of anger, ready to explode at any moment. These are the ones who cut us off in traffic and make an ugly face at us to boot.

The more anonymous our society becomes, the easier it is to speak anger rather than kindness. Some people spout off on e-mail while they're hopping mad, then regret it after the message has arrived at its destination a mere nanosecond later. More than once, I've wished I had a reverse button on my fax machine, so I could "woosh" something back that had already been transmitted. In the old days, we would write a letter to vent our anger, then throw it away—a much better methodology, I think.

Since it is my unedited mouth, and not my carefully edited written words, that get me in trouble, I now have a plan for catching spoken bloopers too. I first stumbled on the germ of this idea in Allen Klein's marvelous book, *The Healing Power of Humor,* then customized it for my peculiar purposes.

You see, having spent ten years immersed in the wilder ways of the world, I had developed a vocabulary that was, shall we say, "colorful." Since I wanted to move past that foolish period of my life and never expose my children to those particular shades of blue, I made a list of the "Ten Things I Could Say, if I Would Say, but I *Won't* Say." Use your imagination.

Then I gave each one of these words or phrases a number, one through ten. Now when the urge to say something less than kind strikes, I let 'em have it: *"Four!"* Sometimes I even flash them all four fingers, which really confuses drivers on the highway. I can read their lips—"What is she saying to me?"—as their faces contort with confusion.

Meanwhile, the kids think this is hysterical. "Boy, Mom is really having a *seven* kind of day!" they'll sing out. It works like a charm. No one is offended, not my children, not God, nor anyone in earshot. Since I've more or less forgotten which number goes with what, I'm not offended either. And, of course, when you behave so ridiculously, you can't help but laugh at yourself.

It's not a perfect solution, but then again, I'm not a perfect woman. Just one who is aiming for the goal set before us: "When she speaks, her words are wise, and kindness is the rule for everything she says" (TLB).

26

Any Way You Slice It . . .

She watches over the ways of her
household, / And does not eat the
bread of idleness.

Proverbs 31:27 NKJV

W hen it comes to watching over our households,
some offspring need watching more than others.
Nancy from Florida has a daughter who was quite
the independent girl at age two. She would get up in the middle
of the night and help herself to anything she could find in the
cabinets or fridge. They finally had to put a rope around the
refrigerator at night to keep her out (which their friends thought
was hysterical).

Very early one morning, this determined little girl made the
block-and-a-half trek to a convenience store, dressed in her
nightgown with bare feet. At 7:00 A.M., Nancy was awakened by
a police officer knocking at her front door, daughter in tow. "I
was totally speechless and very embarrassed, while my two-
year-old was very proud of herself and smiled the whole time!
As the officer was leaving, he advised me that I owed the
convenience store fifty-nine cents for donuts."

We're watching, we're watching, but sometimes they're too
fast for us!

Warning! This Section Includes Tips and Ideas

If you're going to watch over your household, you might as well do it in the most efficient manner possible. Kate Redd's book *52 Timesavers for On-The-Go Moms* is the perfect book for those of us who actually *like* lists, tips, and practical how-to ideas on getting it all done. (True Confession: I enjoy them myself occasionally and was relieved to discover I was already following some of her good suggestions.)

These are the ideas she offers that I know from experience are winners:

- Keep one big calendar (I make photocopies for Bill, fridge, and purse)

- Order from catalogs (this can be dangerous; I'm in a "toss before opening" probation period right now)

- Cluster appointments (why blow a whole morning for just one trip?)

- Streamline grocery shopping (my computerized list comes in handy here)

- Choose child-friendly places (we know 'em all, and they know us!)

- Have a back-up childcare plan (what mom in her right mind wouldn't?)

- Choose no-fuss clothing (if only I didn't find such nice things in rayon!)

One word of caution: a book like that can push our guilt meter up a notch. "I should be doing *all* these things," we think, "starting immediately!" Relax. Choose *one* idea that appeals to your current needs the most and try it for three weeks. Hide such a book until you've mastered, altered, or discarded that plan, then try one new one. Little steps add up to big leaps, eventually.

Patricia Sprinkle, author of *Women Who Do Too Much,* said, "God doesn't want you busy about everything, but He does want you busy about something. He even knows what it is."[1] Which makes me want to shout to the heavens, "What *is* it, Lord?!" To which he would probably say, "Stay tuned, Liz."

"Enjoy Them while They're Young"

Patience not being one of my strong suits, I found the first few months of motherhood, of "watching over" the newest addition to our household, to be exhausting. Of course, well-meaning souls who observed my bloodshot eyes and down-turned mouth told me two things:

1. **"Enjoy this time."**

   Give me a break. What's so enjoyable about infants who stay up all night, cry nonstop, constantly demand food, and have erratic mood swings?

2. **"It will never be like this again."**

   Hogwash. When kids become teenagers, they do the very same things only louder.

My friends mean to comfort and encourage me, I know, but what I really needed was an understanding mother to say, "You're right, it's beastly in the beginning, but soon it will be much better, I promise. Why don't you take a nap, and I'll watch your baby for an hour and clip his little nails while I'm at it?" Bless you, Pat, who did just that.

Of course, now that my children are long past this stage, what did I find myself saying to a young mother yesterday, who was holding a screaming infant and looking frazzled? "Oh, enjoy this time, because it will never be like this again!"

Debbie from Kansas would know better than to say such a thing. She was eight months pregnant and full of baby when her two-year-old crawled under a locked stall in the public rest room at the mall. She couldn't bend down, she couldn't crawl under.

All she could do was "watch over." After much talking and coaxing, her voice became more stern. "Shane, come out of there now!" she insisted. Much to her embarrassment, he replied loudly, "No, you'll knock me over like you did yesterday!"

Some of us, like Rebecca from Kentucky, yearn for "more rainbows" and "fewer clouds." With kids, you get both, usually at the same time.

Fresh from the Oven

Bill is the breadmaker in our family. It's therapy, he tells me as he kneads away at the dough. Plus you can serve it with soup.

But the kind of bread that's described in this verse isn't fit to eat. The Amplified translation draws out its true meaning: the bread of idleness is "gossip, discontent, and self-pity." Only Garfield might find that edible, since he once declared, "I'm tired of being bored, I think I'll make a lateral move to self-pity." That's the bread of idleness, all right.

In *A Mother's Heart,* author Jean Fleming included a list she wrote in her diary when her children were younger:

"What Bothers Me about Being a Mother"

1. The demands on my time

2. Serving them over and over

3. Never finishing my work

4. Frustration of not knowing how to handle problems

5. No time for my interests[2]

She hastened to add that this wasn't good, it was just the truth. I can almost hear the whine in her words because I've said every one myself.

Sometimes, in spite of our imaginary halos, we serve up the bread of idleness to our families. At our house, it culminates in a sound I make that we've all agreed would qualify as Power Whining. Call it what you will—grumbling, complaining, or permanent PMS—it is dangerous stuff and can infect an entire household in the time it takes to tear open a package of Pop Tarts.

Maybe the sound at your house could be described as "yammering." To yammer is "to whine or complain in a loud voice." Oh yes, I've done that. I've even gone around feeling disgruntled, which is odd because when I'm in a good mood, I never say I'm feeling gruntled!

"B-O-R-I-N-G!"

Sometimes, like Garfield, we're just bored with ourselves, and we've allowed that frustration to seep into everything we do. Sharon from Utah still laughs about the day her son Mike came running through the door on the last day of school, having just finished the third grade. After going out to lunch to celebrate with his siblings and playing a board game with Mom, he sat in front of the television for a total of three minutes, tumbled off the couch, stretched, rolled his eyes, and announced, "This is the most boring summer I have ever had!"

> *She watches over the ways of her household, / And does not eat the bread of idleness.*

Kids aren't the only ones who can get bored with the routine of life. We know that our mates might be happier if we stopped nibbling on that bread of idleness. Ellen Glasgow wisely observed that "the only difference between a rut and a grave is their dimensions." If we've dug ourselves into a rut and are feasting on "stale bread," it's time to climb out and find some healthier food.

Leslie said her husband would be so proud of her if she "didn't mope around," and Sandy admitted she should probably "quit nagging!" Another woman knew just what she wanted less of in her life: "Less poor pitiful me and less laziness."

Pet Cemetery III

Which brings us to Fran from Ohio, who knows her husband

would be happier if she'd "stop complaining about our dog and learn to love her." A true mark of sacrifice, that.

Linda from Missouri admits it has not been a great year for pets at her house either.

It began with our four-year-old goldfish leaping to his death from the bowl. Then the dog got hit by a car after he made his break from the "big house" in his quest to mark every bush on the block.

Next, my daughter's birds mistakenly thought their food bowl was a nest, began laying their eggs in their bird seed, then proceeded to peck them open. The lady at the pet store said they would do that if they felt their eggs weren't safe. They probably didn't, with the cat trying to pull the cage down on a daily basis.

Finally, my daughter's prized hamster got loose one night, and the dog licked it to death. At 5:00 A.M. I opened the bathroom door, and the light fell on the hamster's lifeless body. If I had stepped on that thing in the dark, I think I might have joined it in hamster heaven. I couldn't find a shoebox for it, so I put it in a big butter bowl with a lid, and turned the fridge into a hamster morgue until I found time to bury it that evening. I still don't understand why the girls wouldn't eat dinner.

For Linda's sake, when it comes to "watching over the ways of our household," I hope they didn't mean pets too. May the hamster, the eggs, and the goldfish rest in peace.

27

It's Never Too Late to Have a Happy Motherhood

Her children rise up and call her blessed.

Proverbs 31:28 NKJV

To be blessed, according to the Amplified Bible, is to be "happy, fortunate, and to be envied." My mother may have been happy and might have considered herself fortunate. But I did not envy her.

The last day I saw my mother alive was Mother's Day 1978. Four days later, she was gone, a victim of emphysema. For the next nine years, Mother's Day was the most painful day of the year for me, followed closely by every other holiday. No matter what your age, when your mother dies, part of you dies with her.

Yet, at the same time, something was born inside me too. I began to realize that motherhood, the role I had scorned through my teen years, the job I never wanted, might be a pretty special task after all. My longing to be reunited with her was a constant reminder that mothers are one-of-a-kind VIPs. It was then that the desire to become a mother was born in my heart.

The seeds were also planted for another harvest to come: to

finally know God, my heavenly Parent, in a real and personal way. At Mom's funeral, I sang her favorite hymn, "Jesus Makes My Heart Rejoice," though in truth I had no heart knowledge of him at all at that time. It would be four more years before the words of that hymn—"I'm his sheep and know his voice"— would ring true in my heart.

My mother's death, then, led to rebirth for me. Thank you, Mom. Again. Still. "Her children rise up"—wake up, grow up, stand up, speak up, even sing out—"and call her blessed."

The Turning Point

So it was that in 1987, it was my turn to be a mother. That May, on Mother's Day, I was six months pregnant and delighted to finally be able to celebrate that special day again. When the mothers in church were asked to stand up and be recognized, I thought I was far enough along to at least raise my hand (besides, getting up took me six or seven ungraceful minutes!)

Matthew's birth in August 1987 made it official, and I had a new set of letters behind my name: Liz Curtis Higgs, MOM. Twenty months later, in April 1989, God gave me Lillian and probably "smiled at the future" a bit himself. I had just given birth to my mother's pronouncement: "Someday I hope you have a daughter who is *just like you!*"

Now that both have reached school age, I'm breathing again, sleeping better, and waiting for them to "rise up and bless me." How long does this take? Maybe King Lemuel's mother meant her *grand*children would do the rising and the blessing. Maybe when our kids have kids, that's when they'll understand all we've sacrificed for them. As Jennifer from Utah wrote, "The older my children become the more love I feel for my parents. I appreciate my mother more every day."

See, they come around eventually.

Her Children Rise up and Call
Her *Stressed*

An eight-year-old boy in Illinois literally "rose up" to bless his mother, Debbie. He was entranced by Mary Poppins and her magical umbrella, so one day while Mom was at work, Dad was playing golf, and his fifteen-year-old sister was in charge, "He took an umbrella up to the roof of our house and jumped off to see if he could fly. The umbrella reversed and he came crashing to the ground. Scared his sister to death! But a few sutures and he was good as new." Good thing Mom was a nurse and had seen such things before.

When I asked women what they wanted more of and less of in their lives, one woman wanted "more vacations!" but "less stress from family members." For my money, few things can be more stressful than vacations with family! Maxine from Iowa shared her experiences on a family camping trip.

> Here we were in a Winnebago, packed to the gills—three kids, a dog, and a ten-pound sack of potatoes that immediately broke loose and started rolling around. Two miles out of town, the kids opened up a jumbo bottle of Hawaiian punch, we hit a bump, and dumped sixty-four ounces of red punch all over the carpet. A sign of things to come. That evening we stopped at Jellystone Park. It was 101 degrees as we swam in a tiny pool with a thousand campers, watched outdoor 16mm movies, and slept body to body on our camper's dining room table—and the kids loved it!

Meanwhile, how do moms keep going? When I asked women to complete the sentence, "The one thing that makes mothering worth the effort is . . . " Shelley replied, "*Nothing.* It's just that you fall in love with them before you know what an effort they are and you *want* to do everything for them." That's God's wisdom at work: they are so loveable and so needy that they melt the heart of their mother beyond all recognition.

Every woman has different "buttons" her children push that release a fresh wave of Mother Love in her heart. For Kathy, it's "seeing them turn into people I like to be with." Kabee loves "watching my child sleep." I like that, too, because they are, for the moment, quiet! I find myself sneaking into their bedrooms almost every night to catch a glimpse of my two sleeping cuties. Like Kathy said, "One look at their faces and it's all worth it!"

"Whoever Humbles Himself as This Little Child . . ."

Jo from Colorado loves "hearing their prayers." Specifically, Barbara from Illinois has fond memories of the night she was praying with her three-year-old son. They'd had his favorite dish for supper that night—macaroni and cheese. He remembered to thank God in his prayers for the yummy casserole, "But (pause) I don't know how we'll get your dish back to you."

My Matthew learned the power of prayer soon after his sixth birthday. I was tooling into the family room, which is one step down from the hall landing, except I didn't step down onto carpet. I stepped onto a six-inch rubber ball, which sent me skating around for several wild seconds before I tumbled to the floor with a mighty thud, tossing my armload of books in every direction.

Matthew's eyes were wide with horror. Not only had he just witnessed his mother flailing about like a Raggedy Ann doll on roller skates, but now she was on the floor, groaning in pain, and unable to move her ankle. Worst of all, it was *his* rubber ball that had put this disaster in motion, which must mean it was *all his fault!*

I bit my lip to keep from crying and upsetting him even more, but I knew he could see the pain in my eyes when I said, "Go get Pam, honey, tell her Mama is hurt." Out to the office he dashed, returning with a frantic Pam just moments later. She took one look, and headed to the freezer for ice, while Matthew dropped to the floor in a heap, crying for all he was worth.

"It's not your fault, sweet boy. Mama will be fine," I kept

saying, stroking his hair. "I just twisted my ankle, nothing is broken, nothing is bleeding, I'll be okay." He was not convinced, and frankly, neither was I. My ankle was throbbing, and even the thought of standing up made me dizzy. With each moment, the pain was getting worse. Tears keep slipping out of the corner of my eyes.

With Pam's help, and none too gracefully, I made my way to the chair and sank down in its soft cushions while she pulled the ottoman underneath the afflicted ankle, which she wrapped in a bag of ice. "Mom, what can I do, what can I do?" Matthew sobbed, his cheeks wet with fresh tears. "You can give me a big hug," I said, reaching out as he buried his wheat-colored hair in my chest.

Pam seized the opportunity to help Matthew (and me) handle all this. "Matthew, how about if you pray for your mom's ankle? She has a speech tomorrow in Atlanta and she'll need to be able to walk through the airport, so let's start praying right now that it will get better."

I wish I'd had a tape recorder handy, because this young man put his little hands on my ankle and prayed a prayer that would've made angels swoon. His words were so sincere, his faith was so pure, that instantly I knew that his prayers would be answered. To assist in the healing process, I kept my antsy self planted in that chair all evening as Matthew added more ice and more fervent prayers to my ankle. By the next morning, the swelling was completely gone and the pain was minimal, so off to Atlanta I went. Matthew was beaming all over as I thanked him for his special help. "Hey, Mom!" he said, giving me the thumbs up sign, "Prayer works!" Indeed. The words of Isaiah rang in my heart as I headed out the door, blinking away tears: "And a little child shall lead them" (Isa. 11:6 NKJV).

Kids *Do* Say the Darndest Things!

Marcia loves their "sticky kisses and sweaty hugs," while Jacki enjoys "hearing them say 'I love you' and not ask for money in the same breath!" Every mother knows how Dawn Marie feels "when they say or do something that just makes your heart sing," though with my Lillian, more often than not, she makes my heart laugh! Soon after her fifth birthday, as "my" holiday approached, Lillian asked me, "What are you getting me for Mother's Day?" I reminded her that was the one day of the year when presents were supposed to flow in my direction. "But you wouldn't even *be* a mother if it weren't for me!" she said, stomping her foot. She does that a lot. Can't imagine where she got it.

The honesty of children produces amusing results. One day a group of us moms gathered in the first-grade classroom for an awards ceremony, and one of the children called out for all the class to hear, "Oh, Look! Mrs. Blake has make-up on!" Whereupon a dozen young girls began cheering and dancing about while Mrs. Blake turned the color of her blush.

Her children rise up and call her blessed.

Children really do have an opinion about our appearance. Judith from Florida wore her hair very short back in the '60s, but bought a long hairpiece to wear to a party. When her three-year-old son saw her sporting that glamorous new hairdo, he squealed with delight, "Mom! You're a *girl!*"

Darla tells the tale of a grocery shopping trip: "As we were going down the soft drink aisle, three-year-old Lindsey yelled at the top of her little lungs, 'Hey Mom, let's get some gingivitis!'" (Make that ginger ale.)

Cheri from Washington's six-year-old niece was headed to the barn to bed down her new pony when she asked, "How does my pony know when to get up in the morning?" Aunt Cheri explained that "animals have alarm clocks inside of them that tell them when to go to bed, when to get up, and when to eat." The little girl was quiet for a few moments, pondering this information, then she asked, "Do they have night lights too?"

Not All Fun and Games

Being a mother has many fun moments, but sometimes it's just plain work. Having held down at least one job, if not two or three at a time, since 1970, I am here to say that as jobs go, mothering is the hardest one of all. The work schedule is grueling (twenty-four hours a day, seven days a week), the pay is nonexistent (in fact, it's the only job you pay to do), and the benefits can seem few and far between.

Bonnie spoke from the heart when she confessed, "Mothering does not seem worth the effort during the teen years." To her, and all of us, I offer these words of wisdom from Renee: "Eventually they become nice human beings!" Eventually.

Of this I am certain. None of my earthly activities—not my writing, not my speaking, not my singing, not my teaching—none of those "good works" carry the eternal significance that mothering does. One hundred years from now, when I am long gone to glory, no one will be listening to my tapes or telling my funny stories. (I hate the thought of it, but it's true!) Yet, the Lord willing, my children's children's children will be doing wonderful things on this earth *if* the love I have for my young ones today has been communicated, demonstrated, acted upon, and passed on to future generations. As Josh Billings once said, "To bring up a child in the way he should go, travel that way yourself once in a while."

Shirley captures a sense of her calling: "My children are gifts from God. Doing my best with his help is something that makes me feel whole." Cynde delights in seeing her children "grow to become beautiful souls!" For Ruth, what makes mothering worthwhile is "seeing your children blossom into mature, caring adults with successful marriages and faith in God."

"Give Me Patience, Lord . . . *Now!*"

Children, by their very nature and existence, test us as human beings. As one mother phrased it, "When you have a child, you learn a *lot* about your emotional range. Parent and child are bound by emotion, not intelligence."[1]

In becoming a mother, I discovered that all those nasty little character flaws that I'd learned to hide so well from my friends and coworkers came out at night when I got home. My lack of patience and lack of discipline would be the two most glaring shortcomings I'd mention first.

What a comfort to read hundreds of surveys that all said the same thing as women put into words those imperfections we all identify with:

"As a mother, I'm not so good at . . ."
"Being patient with noise and silliness"
"Taking time out to play"
"Always controlling my temper"
"Recognizing their individuality"
"Relaxing my standards for them"
"Really listening to them"
"Disciplining the kids consistently"
"Remembering to praise them"
"Trusting myself as a good mother"

(Note the names were not included—I'm here to *encourage*, not discourage!)

There were also moms like Linda who fretted at her inability to "keep dental appointments," or Isabel's concern over her lack of skill at "hosting pajama parties." What *all* the mothers seemed to share was the ability to laugh at their less-than-perfect selves, which in my opinion is the key ingredient to good mothering: a sense of humor!

Karyn from Missouri was intent on helping her sons develop positive self-esteem. When she would hear them belittling themselves ("I'm so stupid," "I'm ugly," "I can't do anything right") she would give them a special hand signal, and they would begrudgingly change their tune to "I'm very smart, I'm very talented, I can do anything I put my mind to, and I love myself." One morning when she was getting ready for a community conference that she was in charge of, she was mentally reviewing the day's activities:

A thought began to gnaw at me: "Does the meeting start at 9:30 or 8:30?" Surely, I would have remembered. Still, the doubts hung on. I climbed from the shower and phoned my co-coordinator. Her husband answered, "Cyndi's long gone. The conference started an hour ago." My worst fears snapped to reality. How could I have committed such an oversight? I screamed at my children, "Throw on your clothes—quick! We gotta go, *now!*"

Splashing on my make-up, I was muttering aloud, "I'm such an idiot. I don't deserve to be in charge. What a dumb thing to do . . ." While I rambled on, verbally kicking myself, my youngest son walked up, put his hands gently around my face, locked his gaze with mine and said, "You're beautiful, you're smart, you're talented, you can do anything you put your mind to, and *we love you!*"

Always and Forever

The reality is, our children rise up and bless us every day, if we're listening. Judy delights in hearing, "I love you, Mommy." Jo rejoices when she sees "the light in their eyes when they learn something new." Kelly draws strength from those "hugs at the end of a frustrating day."

As Jean Fleming wrote, a mother is "a woman of influence. I impart values, stimulate creativity, develop compassion, modify weaknesses, and nurture strengths. I can open life up to another individual. And I can open an individual up to life."[2]

While I cannot rise up and bless my mother, I can honor her memory by giving my best effort to mothering my own children. Not by being a perfect mother, nor necessarily a patient mother, nor by any means a totally disciplined mother, but certainly by being a mother who loves God, her husband, and her children, and looks for as many ways as possible to communicate to them, "I'm glad you are part of my world!"

28
Husband Sings Wife's Praises! Film at 11:00

~

... Her husband also, and he praises
her: / "Many daughters have done
well, / But you excel them all."

Proverbs 31:28b-29 NKJV

While reading a local small-town newspaper, my eyes were drawn to an unusual advertisement, which in large print said: "Hubert and Larry are proud to say that their wives, Brenda and Kaye, are finally playing Rook better. They won a few games over the weekend. It's about time!"

Gentlemen, this is not what was meant by rising up and saying, "You excel them all."

If most husbands knew how little it takes to make us feel loved and appreciated, I believe they would say kind things more often. Flowers and chocolate have their place, but a daily (hourly?) dose of praise would be the best gift of all. It doesn't have to be much. "Thank you for folding my undershirts," would be a great start. "I noticed you scrubbed out the tub," sounds good. How about, "I'll cook all weekend"? Now *that* would be music to our waiting ears!

Productive Praise

Sandy from Pennsylvania is willing to skip the roses, romance, and "rise and shine" compliments. "Actions speak louder than words," she wrote, "and when the dear blessed soul is out there on an icy morning warming up my car and scraping ice so I can go to work, *that's* romantic as far as this kid's concerned. Even though 'only angels can wing it,' there *are* some 'angels' out there who have baseball caps instead of wings!"

When some of us conjured up our image of the perfect husband, it was how he demonstrated love, rather than how he vocalized it, that spoke the loudest. Jeanine from Michigan was hoping for a little of both: "Sensitive at the right times and strong at the right times."

Well, I think I found him! Among the letters, stories, and surveys I received from hundreds of women, I also received one story from a married man in Connecticut, who quit his job of ten years and agreed to move to a new town, buy their first house, and take care of their brand-new daughter Katie. He wrote: "I spent two years at home with our daughter while my wife remained at her job at a local hospital. I did all the 'Mommy' things like the YMCA pool, gym class, shopping, and so on. I coupon-shopped, compared diaper brands, struggled with laundry, and went to Discovery Toy Parties."

Raise your hands if you'd like us to explore a possible cloning of this fine gentleman. His version of "rising up and blessing his wife" was not only to speak well of her, but also to support her in dozens of other practical, hands-on, productive ways.

"You Don't Have to Be Crazy to Live Here But . . ."

Sharon from Michigan, tongue firmly in cheek, thinks her husband might sing her praises more if he were married to "Bo Derek instead of Erma Bombeck." Funny, because at our house, Bill would go for Erma in a heartbeat. What a woman! Humor in the household means a greater potential for the sharing of grace, forgiveness, even sincere praise. When I moan that the house isn't clean enough, that dinner wasn't tasty enough, that my body isn't firm enough, Bill gently reminds me that he didn't marry Martha Stewart or Jane Fonda. "Just be yourself, Liz," he always says. "After all, that *is* who I married." (I think that's supposed to be a compliment!)

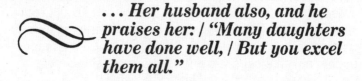

... Her husband also, and he praises her: / "Many daughters have done well, / But you excel them all."

The sense of humor and play that many of us try to bring to our marriage relationships has some of our husbands literally jumping for joy. The following story requires a little background.

Toni and Ellen were two outrageously fun women I met at a retreat in southern California. One evening, they were sitting in their hotel room, and Ellen was a little discouraged. Toni got this crazy idea (she does that regularly) to start jumping up and down on the bed. "I'll bet you were good at this as a kid!" she said to Ellen, coaxing her to give it a try.

Soon, Ellen got on her own bed and gave a little jump. Then a bigger one. Pretty soon, both women were leaping with child-like abandon, with their hands cradled over their heads in case they hit the ceiling! An hour later, exhausted from all the aerobic laughing and leaping, they collapsed in a heap. Ellen was, to say the least, no longer in the doldrums.

But it doesn't stop there. Toni went home "and explained the art of bed-jumping to my reserved husband and my very cool high-school-aged son. It only took a five-minute demonstration before we were all on the queen-sized bed together. What joy and laughter entered that room!

"When my husband's heart rate slowed, he said that he had forgotten what it felt like to be alive, and that it was a wonderful feeling. 'Life is *fun* again!' burst from my son's lips as he headed for his room for the night. The lesson for me in all of this is that it is life's simple pleasures that bring us the greatest joy."

Amen, Toni!

She added, "P.S. We are up to twelve different ways to jump on the bed and are working on dismounts!"

"Rise Up" and Buy Us Presents, Please

Some of us like to watch our husbands jump for joy over our contribution to their lives.

Some women desire romantic expressions of praise: candlelight dinners, beautiful flowers, soft music, green cash.

Others among us like to see more practical expressions of admiration: lawns mowed, weeds pulled, floors mopped, dishes done. We're talking above and beyond their usual "Honey Do" list, naturally.

Still others would be content if their husbands just got them what they requested for Christmas! Patricia from Ohio remembers her first yuletide season with her husband, twenty-two years ago:

It was a holiday of high expectations. I had hinted, none too subtly, about my desire for a bronze wall hanging. You remember how popular they were—three-dimensional scenes of an outdoor European cafe or a young boy flying a kite in a field. I'd shown them to my husband in stores and catalogs, had the wall picked out, and really didn't care which scene I received.

Under the tree a week before Christmas was a box—three feet long, three feet high, six inches wide. My wall hanging! It was going to be a grand holiday.

Finally, on Christmas morning I confessed to my husband that I knew what my gift was and I could hardly wait to see what scene he'd chosen. He gave me a funny look, like he wished I hadn't guessed.

When it came time to open our presents, I began ripping the gift wrap off the box. Clearly printed on the side of the carton was "Folding Laundry Cart with Wheels."

"Hah!" I laughed, "You've tried to fool me by putting it in this box!" In my frenzied tearing of paper to get into the box, I missed his growing look of despair.

My husband remembers 1972 as the coldest winter on the family record. The wall remained bare for months.

Of course, the story has a happy ending. Twenty years later, she was still using the laundry cart on wheels. And, for Christmas 1973, her husband was sent to the mall with ten index cards, listing the item, color, size, store, department, clerk's name, *and* a picture. Patricia assures us, "He's never again had trouble finding that perfect gift!"

Faint Praise . . . Very Faint

Our surveys told us that for lots of us, our husbands serve as role models in our family lives. Gayle from Montana said, "It's because he's very patient and even with our kids." Sue mentioned her husband's "patience and encouragement." Doris appreciates "his calmness and ability to see beyond the immediate." And Marilynn says she plain "lucked out!"

I'm not certain that Debbie from Illinois felt very lucky about her husband's involvement in this little family escapade:

Early one cold, rainy spring day, my husband, three children, and I went off to the woods to hunt mushrooms. We didn't find many mushrooms, but we did find a three-foot green snake. After much screaming, shrieking, and chasing each other with this snake dangling from a stick, the kids killed the snake with the stick and put it in a paper sack.

During the twenty-minute ride home, the dead snake rode in the floor of the car by the heater. As we neared Grandma's house, I opened the sack and out shot the much-alive snake, rigid as a yardstick!

It was like a Chinese fire drill. The car stopped dead in the middle of the street, all four doors opened simultaneously, and out tumbled my husband (all 230 pounds of him), me, and three screaming teenagers. After we composed ourselves and caught the snake, the whining began.

"Can we keep the snake? All boys need a snake for a pet. Do you want us to grow up to be sissies?" We had a lot less company after Mr. Green joined our family.

I'm sure her husband patted Debbie on the back for being a "good sport," one of the greatest compliments some men ever give. But it might have been less traumatic if he'd just said, "There are many fine women in the world, but you are the best of them all!" (Prov. 31:29 TLB).

29
Charm School Is for Snakes

Charm is deceitful and beauty is passing, /
But a woman who fears the LORD, she
shall be praised.

Proverbs 31:30 NKJV

No one I know ever went to charm school, but I still grew up knowing what such places were, in theory: a place to develop manners, to learn which fork to use first, how to sit correctly, and maybe even how to curtsy (which obviously I don't know how to do properly, since I just had to use a dictionary to find out how to spell it!).

Thanks to this verse in Proverbs, excellent women like us are excused from attending charm school, because every translation agrees: "Charm is deceptive."

In the Hebrew, *charm* means "showing favor for your own gain." Having a hidden agenda, as we would say. We know this kind of woman. She has talked us into baking cookies, carpooling kids, and lugging lawn chairs out for picnics we didn't even want to attend, let alone host.

When they say "flattery will get you everywhere," that's the kind of charm we're talking about. I, for one, prefer to never give or receive that sort of charm again. Picture a snake charmer, and it should cure us of ever wanting to be known as charming.

Think of those telephone solicitors, who call us right in the middle of dinner and say cheerfully, "Hello! How are you this evening?" They remain charming as all get out until it becomes clear that you are not going to give them what they want: a signature on a lifetime contract for lawn care service. Suddenly, that overly cheerful, friendly sound is gone from their voice. "You mean you are going to let aphids take over your lawn?!"

Bill received a call from a woman trying to sell him long-distance service recently. As she went happily along, doing a sing-song rendition of the obvious script before her, Bill finally interrupted her and said, "Ma'am, I'm afraid I don't have time for this conversation right now, I'm very busy." The charming chatter abruptly quit, replaced by a cool voice that said, "We are not having a conversation, Mr. Higgs, I am telling you about my product."

That's what this verse means by, "charm is deceptive" (NIV). It looks and sounds like one thing but is another completely. In the Hebrew, it means "falsehood, disappointment," literally "molten wax," an imitation of the real thing.

Those of us who are in sales can learn something from our proverbial sister. Charm does not lead to sales . . . it leads to lost revenue!

Beauty Is As Beauty Does

Fine, we don't have to be charming, just sincere. But beautiful . . . now *that* would be fun, if only for a weekend. Just to stroll through the grocery aisles and have someone say, "Wow!" instead of "Do you know where the Ultra Slim Fast is?" Oh, please.

Most of us look in the mirror and see what American humorist George Ade observed: "Her features did not seem to know the value of teamwork."

By fashion magazine standards, I've probably only met two or three flawlessly beautiful women, face to face, in my lifetime. (I tried not to stand too close to them.)

But by the standards of *real* beauty—a woman who celebrates the face and figure she has today, adorns it in style and taste, and gets on with life—there are thousands of beautiful women. My guess is, the woman holding this book is one of them!

In my own life, I've come to a place of peace about my abundant body and would encourage you with all my heart to do the same with whatever size and shape you may be. Minnie Smith took the words right out of my mouth: "I am as my Creator made me, and since He is satisfied, so am I."

My next challenge, as it is for many of us, is to embrace the inevitability of time and its effects on our forty-plus bodies. As Faith Baldwin expressed it, "Time is a dressmaker specializing in alterations."

No Fear of Forty

For the record, I turned forty in July 1994. The ground did not shake. Parts of me did, of course, but they shook when I was thirty-nine too. Author Susan Katz read my mind (or looked at my body!) when she wrote, "I feel the tug, my flesh molding itself to gravity; closer now to the soil than ever to the sky."[1]

A friend sent me an encouraging list of reasons why we should look forward to turning forty based on statistical evidence. For example, the over-forty woman will be less likely to divorce, more immune to colds, and less likely to spend time in a penitentiary. We need an hour's less sleep than we did at twenty and are less likely to develop mental instability. Isn't that comforting?

Of the many fun cards I received on my Big Day, a favorite has to be from my sister Sarah (who crossed over that line a long time ago). It said: "Look at the bright side of being forty—you've already had as much fun as two twenty-year-olds!"

Actually, my thirty-ninth birthday was much more traumatic: all that angst about leaving behind another decade, all those Jack Benny jokes (most of which I told myself), all that ribbing all year long, "Thirty-nine? Oh, sure you are!"

Lin from Ohio remembers the day before her own thirty-ninth birthday. She was seated at a child-size table, stapling together some papers for her young students. The stapler jammed then suddenly opened and staples flew everywhere.

She wrote, "We cleaned them all up and got back to business

when five-year-old Carson said, 'Mrs. G., there's a staple in your hair.' I brushed at it, but nothing fell out. 'It's still there!' he said. I brushed again, but still nothing. He insisted, 'Well, there's something silver up there!'" Indeed.

I really don't mind gray hairs. I married a silver-maned man, and I rather enjoy finding a few grays in my own hair, since the Bible clearly states, "The silver-haired head is a crown of glory" (Prov. 16:31 NKJV). Such encouragement! No, it's not the gray hair that bothers me, it's the hair that's disappearing altogether that I'm not happy about. My doctor assures me that all is well, it's just hormonal and hereditary. A little thinning out on top, no big deal.

Watch my lips: it's a big deal when it's my hair! I've teased, sprayed, moussed, swallowed vitamins, rubbed in conditioners and scalp treatments, and read the Rogaine ads very closely. All to no avail. Welcome to your forties, Liz. Remember how in your teen years, you prayed for "thin"? Ta-da.

Ripe for the Picking and Grinning

I could handle hair falling out of the top of my head, if at the same time it hadn't started poking out of my chin and neck! Good grief, where did those come from? I speak to women's health groups all the time and have never in all of their literature even found a reference to "forty fuzz." What a nuisance. Now I've got to carry tweezers with my lipstick.

We have to look at it like the beautiful Brigitte Bardot does: "It is sad to grow old but nice to ripen." Fine, if you are shaped like a young pear, which takes forever to turn ripe and takes on a golden sheen when it does. Not so good if you are a banana, which has no shape at all, ripens in about three days, and turns dark and mushy.

We heard from Sandy from Hawaii, who recently went through a "hyste-wreck-of-me," and wrote to say "many women need a lot of encouragement and humor when dealing with the influence of estrogen!" Carol hoped to find among these pages, "A light-hearted look at facing life at all ages—middle age and senior years can be overwhelming."

Even more than "face life," let's "embrace life" at any age. And let's move to Florida, where instead of big billboards advertising "Glasses in One Hour," they have billboards for "Dental Express—Same Day Dentures for $199!"

I truly don't mind my body getting older—who has a choice about these things anyway?—but I am fighting to keep my mind young by trying to censor the following phrases *before* they leave my lips . . .

"These younger kids today . . ."

"I remember when . . ."

"Nowadays, they just don't . . ."

"Back in the '60s, we . . ."

If you hear me start to say any of the above, just poke me with my tweezers!

Vanity Not-So-Fair

My mental picture of a vain woman is one standing in front of a mirror, primping and smiling at her narcissistic self. The Hebrew tells a truer tale: *vain* means "something that only lasts a moment."

That's worldly beauty, all right: short-lived! The firm muscle tone and wrinkle-free skin of youth gives way with time, and not much time at that. Mary Anne from South Carolina remembers a visit to her parents' house, when she walked into their bedroom to return a book, right at the same time her dad was changing into his pajamas. With an embarrassed, "Whoops!" she quickly turned around and left the room. Her Dad started to laugh and called out that she'd "almost caught him in his birthday suit."

"Well," she replied, "I'm not sure which suit you were changing into, but it sure needed ironing!"

So, if charm and beauty—the qualities our society finds exceedingly valuable—aren't the trademarks of an excellent woman, what is? We have some ideas, and good ones at that:

"A partner in all matters of the relationship."

"One who has respect for herself and her husband."

"Non-nag, cheerful, creative, helpful, glad to be a woman."

Those of us who seek the timeless, rather than vain, beauty produced by the qualities above will have one happy man on our hands. And, if we are single, we'll have something just as valuable: one happy us!

Scared to Life

Fears and phobias are old news. A little therapy, a little role playing, a deep breath, and onto that airplane we go—or over that bridge, or into that crowd, or whatever fears many women among us may have overcome, or wish to. We're told to "feel the fear and do it anyway."

Although I have few real fears, I'm not crazy about close spaces like a crowded elevator or looking straight down from a very high place. Almost all of us have a fear of appearing foolish. For instance, say I start down the steps leading out of a commuter airplane and accidentally hook the elastic cord from my luggage carrier onto the handrail. I would not only cascade down the airplane steps, but snap back as well. Now, that would be scary. Unintentional bungee jumping, with luggage. Very scary.

But that's not the kind of fear the Proverbs 31 woman had. Not sweaty palms and shaking hands. Nor is it the fear Cybele from Vermont mentioned, when she expressed a desire to have "less fear about taking the 'right' life path." I think we all share a certain amount of that concern.

 Charm is deceitful and beauty is passing, / But a woman who fears the LORD, she shall be praised.

This is "fear of the Lord," which means "to be in awe of, reverent toward." A healthy fear, considering his power. It's a recognition of his magnificence and might which, once grasped, means less fear of anything else. Larry Eisenberg has the right idea: "For peace of mind, resign as general manager of the universe." Why not, the job has already been filled!

For me, to "fear the Lord" means to respect and love God so completely that I want to honor his goodness and grace with my life. While getting my thoughts together for this book, I did a summer Bible study of Proverbs 31, and asked my small but mighty team, "What is your greatest spiritual challenge?" Here's what they said:

"To keep growing in maturity, instead of being too comfortable in my spiritual walk."

"To stay focused on God."

"To have a consistent quiet time."

"To be obedient to God's expressed will for my life."

"To concentrate on producing the fruit of the spirit."

"To have a closer relationship with God in order to survive!"

Singer and author Annie Chapman wrote that "the balanced woman is not out to please some of the people all of the time, or all of the people some of the time. Her strategy for living is to be simply, purely, passionately devoted to the Lord."[2]

On our surveys, I asked a more open-ended question, "What do you wish you had more of in your life?" Some of the same answers came from women from all over America and all walks of life:

"Spiritual awareness"

"Knowledge of the Bible"

"Prayer time"

"Joy of the Lord"

"Time for spiritual growth"

A walk with God is a very private thing indeed, so the honesty of these women is especially generous. Perhaps it could be said of them what author Tony Campolo wrote: "When people recognize God as the ultimate Significant Other, they define their worth in terms of their relationship with Him."[3]

The truth is, that relationship is meaningful to a vast number of people. A 1991 Roper Poll asked a random sampling of men and women, "What is 'success'?" For both men and women, "being a good spouse and parent" was at the top of the list. Second on the list for women was "being true to God," more than twice as important to them as having knowledge, wealth, power, influence, or fame.[4]

There are many in media ministry today, crying out that our nation is going to Hades in a handbasket. And there is no doubt that violence, drug use, family problems, and sexual diseases are on the upsweep. I read and watch the news daily, and so I am not unaware, nor unconcerned.

But then I come back to these verses that offer such hope, that express wise counsel, that give clear direction, and that ultimately provide an exciting promise: "She shall be praised" by her husband, her family, her peers, her community, and her Lord. Once again, I am encouraged.

30

Applause! Applause!

Give her of the fruit of her hands, /
And let her own works praise her in
the gates.

Proverbs 31:31 NKJV

I've always thought that this verse is in the wrong place.
The passage should end with the triumphant conclusion
of verse 30, "She shall be praised!" Then a trumpet blast
and close the book . . . slap! The End. As one commentator
concluded his study of the chapter, "May her number increase
and the praise that belongs to her be heard in gates all over the
world."[1] Brava!

But no, King Lemuel's mother had one more point to make,
and anyway, it was an acrostic, a Hebrew A to Z, and she had to
say *something* that began with the last Hebrew letter, "tau."

Maybe she was feeling guilty about that "husband at the
gates" thing and wanted to assure us that women belong there
too. Maybe she wanted to point out that not only would God
praise this wonderful wife but so would society. The Living Bible
says, "These good deeds of hers shall bring her honor and
recognition from even the leaders of the nations."

Or maybe—just maybe—this is exactly how the passage
needs to end: with applause. After all, every performer waits for

it, prays for it, agonizes over it. "Are they clapping as loudly as last night? Are they standing up?" All of us, from all walks of life, need some public recognition now and again, even if the public is just our circle of friends. As Kitty O'Neill Collins said, "What I'm looking for is a blessing that's *not* in disguise."

Harvest Time

The "ideal woman" of Proverbs not only worked hard, but she also tended to her bottom line, her profits, the fruit of her labors. None of these words point solely to money, of course. In fact, the Amplified version of verse 16 says, "With her savings [of time and strength] she plants fruitful vines in her vineyard."

At Laughing Heart Farm, we plant grapes in our vineyard, but for the sole purpose of making grapevine wreaths. The birds get any grapes that the beetles don't eat first. That's pretty much the story of our whole garden, but at least we can say we followed the biblical command to "work the land," even if we do cheat and buy nursery plants that are already half grown.

The men and women of biblical times knew plenty about planting and harvesting crops, about growing and pruning. There are nearly seventy references to vineyards alone. These days, the closest some of us get to growing and pruning is houseplants. Darlene from Kentucky described growing a beautiful jade plant, which her two-year-old daughter turned into Swiss cheese in a matter of minutes using a ball point pen.

As I felt my anger rise and opened my mouth to let her have it, Kristin started yelling, "It's okay! Mommy, it's okay! See, see I made smiley faces!" Sure enough, on every leaf was carefully poked two eyes, a nose, and a smiley mouth. My anger drained away, and tears over my poor plant mingled with tears of laughter. The plant survived and thrived, ditto for Kristin, and thankfully, so did my sense of humor.

Vines are not the only growing things we care for and not the only things in our lives that bear fruit.

Unexpected Fruit

Sometimes our vineyards bear a painful and bitter fruit, not because of our lack of effort, but because of the weeds that grow up and choke our vines, or because of the seeds from former harvests that sprout up unexpectedly. The following seven women are to be commended for sharing so honestly from their own heartbreaking experiences in the vineyard called Life. To honor their transparency, and protect their privacy, I chose to tell you something about them other than their names.

When asked, "What is the one thing you wish you'd done differently as a mother?" these women said:

"Spent more time trying to educate myself about alcoholism and codependency while I was still married, to help my family."
　　Billing Clerk, age fifty-five, divorced after twenty-three years

"Had better success in keeping my marriages intact for the children's sake."
　　Homemaker, age fifty-one, divorced after twenty-four years

"Quit drinking sooner."
　　Programmer, age forty-two, divorced after twenty years

"Not left their father and broken up their family life, leaving them behind."
　　Hospital office manager, age forty-two, remarried

"Left an abusive marriage while they were young."
　　Nurse, age sixty, divorced after thirty-two years

"Tried harder to get help for a problem child. Our oldest son was killed in a drunk driving accident in 1991."
　　Clerk and student, age forty-one, married

"Kicked out an abusive husband long, long before I did."
　　Secretary, age fifty-one, remarried

There, but for the grace of God, go any of us. My prayer for these women, and millions of others, is for the healing power of love, grace, and laughter to fill their lives once more and bring forth "good fruit" in their vineyards.

Quiet Works, Thunderous Applause

For many years, I've had the honor of serving as master of ceremonies for a long-term healthcare association banquet. Awards are presented in dozens of categories, and the highlight for me is the statewide Adult Volunteer of the Year Award. In 1993, the winner was Marie Merritt of Campbellsville, Kentucky. As always, I was delighted to announce her name and watch her come forward to receive her well-earned award.

Little did I know that two months later, I would be speaking in her church. She came up and introduced herself, and I realized that she was the embodiment of this verse: "Give her the reward she has earned, and let her works bring her praise at the city gate" (NIV). When I came to that verse in my presentation, I asked her to stand and be acknowledged. As soon as I mentioned her name, hundreds of women from her community burst into applause to honor this dear woman who had given so unselfishly of her time to volunteer 1,700+ hours each year at Medco Center.

"After my husband died," she said, "I didn't work for two years and had no money to speak of, so I began going to the nursing home to encourage the folks there. I've never known a time when I didn't have enough gas in my car to get there and back." Her blue eyes shone with the joy that only years of serving God will produce. Billy Graham said, "Someday we will be as perfect as angels are now."[2] I believe Marie has a head start on most of us.

Fruit That Never Spoils

Olive Schreiner said, "And it came to pass that after a time the artist was forgotten, but the work lived." As I look over my forty years of living, and pray for the grace of enjoying forty more, I wonder what the eighty-year old Liz will wish she had done at forty? I believe I can say without hesitation, I will wish I had been more like the Proverbs 31 woman.

Talk about getting your priorities straight! If you look at the whole chapter, she stacked up her life in this order:

God

Family

Church/Community

Work

I think almost any woman who values those four areas of service would probably say the same thing and feel very righteous as she did so. One slight problem. If I put my calendar next to that list of priorities, it is shockingly upside down:

Work:	ten to twelve hours a day
Family:	three hours a day
Church/Community:	twenty minutes a day (on a good day)
God:	five minutes of prayer at the end of the day (?!)

I promised no lists, tips, or ideas, but I didn't promise not to put before us all a goal: to turn our own lists, even our lives, right side up and begin to actually live what we say we believe.

 Give her the fruit of her hands, / And let her own works praise her in the gates.

Someday I hope I can say, along with one of my most respected role models, Erma Bombeck: "When I stand before God at the end of my life, I would hope that I would not have a single bit of talent left and could say, 'I used everything you gave me.'"

The Fabric of Our Lives

Several years ago, the stage play *Quilters* came to Louisville. It is the story of a group of frontier women who traveled across

America with their families, bouncing along in covered wagons, suffering every hardship known to womankind, but surviving. At every tragedy and every celebration, a woman showed up at the door with a quilt in her arms, intoning, "These quilts is from the ladies of the First Baptist Church."[3]

Quilts. They kept their children warm, kept the rain from coming in, and kept the wolf from their door, even when there was no door.

Quilts made from scraps of their lives, lovingly sewn together with a thousand tiny stitches.

Quilts like the one hanging in front of me now with "1890" carefully stitched at the bottom, made of fabrics that have lived longer than most people. Crazy quilts with no pattern at all, or intricate recreations of familiar old patterns—Bear Paw, Lone Star, Log Cabin, or Nine Patch.

Quilts, then and now, are legacies we leave behind for our children to cherish, and better still, to use.

Back to *Quilters*. The play ends, the stage darkens, and then an amazing thing happens, which the script calls "the last unfolding."[4] The fabric-covered stage, a dull, uneven muslin, begins to lift heavenward on invisible wires and the audience gasps aloud. Before them hangs an enormous quilt, the size of the entire stage itself, huge and colorful and altogether beautiful.

The quilt pattern is, appropriately, the Tree of Life. Sarah, the matriarch, reenters the scene and delivers the final line of the play:

> Give her of the fruit of her hands, / And let her own works praise her in the gates.

[Audience applauds. Stage lights out.]

Only Angels Can Wing It

NOTES

Chapter 1

1. Billy Graham, *Angels* (Dallas: Word, 1994), 60.
2. Kevin Leman, *Bonkers* (New York: Dell, 1987), 10–11.
3. Herbert Lockyer, *All the Women of the Bible* (Grand Rapids: Zondervan, 1967), 274.
4. *Webster's New World Dictionary of American English* (New York: Simon & Schuster, 1988), 104.
5. Barbara Walters, quoted in *The Quotable Woman* (Philadelphia: Running Press), 15.
6. Lockyer, *All the Women of the Bible*, 214.
7. Clifton J. Allen, ed., *The Broadman Bible Commentary* (Nashville: Broadman, 1971), 97.
8. Jean Fleming, *A Mother's Heart* (Colorado Springs: NavPress, 1982), 44.

Chapter 2

1. LaJoyce Martin, *Mother Eve's Garden Club* (Sisters: Multnomah, 1993), 157.
2. Jill Briscoe, *Queen of Hearts* (Old Tappan: Fleming H. Revell, 1984), 9.
3. Allen, *The Broadman Bible Commentary*, 98.
4. Martin, *Mother Eve's Garden Club*, 160.

Chapter 3

1. Luci Swindoll, *After You've Dressed for Success* (Waco: Word, 1987), 67.
2. Paula Rinehart, *Perfect Every Time* (Colorado Springs: NavPress, 1992), 34.
3. Virginia Barber and Merrill Maguire Skaggs, *The Mother Person* (New York: Bobbs-Merrill, 1975), 6.
4. Rinehart, *Perfect Every Time*, 44.
5. Peg Rankin, *How to Care for the Whole World and Still Take Care of Yourself* (Nashville: Broadman & Holman, 1994), x.

Chapter 7

1. Dave Barry, *Babies and Other Hazards of Sex* (Emmaus: Rodale Press, 1984), 12.

Chapter 10

1. Shirley Rogers Radl, *Mother's Day Is Over* (New York: Arbor House, 1987), xv.
2. T. Berry Brazelton, M.D., *Working and Caring* (New York: Addison-Wesley, 1987), xviii.

Chapter 12

1. Leman, *Bonkers*, 188.
2. Elaine St. James, *Simplify Your Life* (New York: Hyperion, 1994), 7.
3. Karen Hull, *The Mommy Book* (Grand Rapids: Zondervan, 1986), 198.
4. Melodie M. Davis, *Working, Mothering and Other "Minor" Dilemmas* (Waco: Word, 1984), 62.
5. Elizabeth Cody Newenhuyse, *The Woman with Two Heads* (Dallas: Word, 1991), 51-52.

Chapter 13

1. Beverly Sills, *The Quotable Woman*, 161.
2. Norman Cousins, *Head First: The Biology of Hope* (New York: E.P. Dutton, 1989), 126.

Chapter 14

1. Donna Otto, *The Stay at Home Mom* (Eugene: Harvest House, 1991), 129.
2. Dee Brestin, *The Lifestyles of Christian Women* (Wheaton: Victor Books, 1991), 138.
3. Sirgay Sanger, M.D. and John Kelly, *The Woman Who Works, The Parent Who Cares* (Boston: Little, Brown and Company, 1987), 177.
4. Carroll Stoner, *Reinventing Home* (New York: A Plume Book/Penguin Group, 1991), 235.

Chapter 15

1. Allen, *The Broadman Bible Commentary*, 99.
2. Briscoe, *Queen of Hearts*, 147.
3. Rinehart, *Perfect Every Time*, 15.
4. Ibid., 21.
5. Ibid., 24.
6. Herbert J. Freudenberger and Gail North, *Women's Burnout* (New York: Penguin, 1985), 232-33.
7. Annie Chapman with Maureen Rank, *Smart Women Keep It Simple* (Minneapolis: Bethany House, 1992), 167.

Chapter 16

1. Deborah Fallows, *A Mother's Work* (Boston: Houghton Mifflin, 1985), 234.

Chapter 17

1. Gildna Radner, *It's Always Something* (New York: Avon, 1990), 205.

Chapter 20

1. Erma Bombeck, *The Erma Bombeck 1992 Desk Calendar* (Kansas City: Andrews & McMeel, A Universal Press Syndicate, 1992), 2 March, Monday.

Chapter 21

1. Layne Longfellow, *Beyond Success: When Ambition's No Longer Enough* (Prescott: Lecture Theatre, Inc., 1993), audio cassette.

Chapter 22

1. Brenda Hunter, *Where Have All the Mothers Gone?* (Grand Rapids: Zondervan, 1982), 120.
2. Patricia Aburdene and John Naisbitt, *Megatrends for Women* (New York: Villard, 1992), 229.
3. Hull, *The Mommy Book,* 194-98.
4. Bebe Moore Campbell, *Successful Women, Angry Men* (New York: Random House, 1986), 19.
5. Katherine Wyse Goldman, *My Mother Worked and I Turned Out Okay* (New York: Villard Books, 1993), 4.

Chapter 23

1. Peter Guber, quoted in Jo Ann Larsen's "Family Corner" column in the *Deseret News,* Salt Lake City, 20 February 1994.
2. Kate Halverson, *The Quotable Woman,* 34.

Chapter 24

1. Bonnie Altenhein, *How Angels Get Their Wings* (New York: Wings Books, 1994).
2. "The Birth of Laughter," *The Laughter Prescription Newsletter,* Box 7985, Northridge, California.
3. Bette Midler, *The Quotable Woman,* 39.
4. Joel Goodman, "Jay Leno's Planet," *Laughing Matters,* Vol. 5, No. 4, 140.
5. Allen, *The Broadman Bible Commentary,* 98–99.
6. Cal Samra, *The Joyful Christ* (San Francisco: Harper & Row, 1986), 8.

Chapter 26

1. Patricia H. Sprinkle, *Women Who Do Too Much* (Grand Rapids: Zondervan, 1992), 29.
2. Fleming, *A Mother's Heart,* 147-48.

Chapter 27

1. Barber and Skaggs, *The Mother Person,* 204.
2. Fleming, *A Mother's Heart,* 27.

Chapter 29

1. Susan A. Katz, "New Directions," *When I Am Old I Shall Wear Purple* (Watsonville: Papier-Mache Press, 1987), 71.
2. Chapman, *Smart Women Keep It Simple,* 15.

3. Tony Campolo, *The Success Fantasy* (Wheaton: Victor Books, 1980), 109.
4. The Roper Organization Poll, as reported in *The Hope Heart Newsletter,* The Hope Heart Institute, Seattle, Washington, 1991, 8.

Chapter 30
1. Allen, *The Broadman Bible Commentary,* 99.
2. Graham, *Angels,* 45.
3. Molly Newman and Barbara Damashek, *Quilters* (New York: Dramatists Play Service, Inc., 1986), 52.
4. Ibid., 59.

About the Author

After a decade of traveling up and down the dial as a popular radio personality in five states, Liz Curtis Higgs moved out of the studio and onto the stage in 1987 as a conference and retreat speaker. Since then, she has logged more than 700 presentations for businesses, hospitals, churches, and associations in 43 states.

Her writing career officially began in 1993 with the publication of two books: *Does Dinner in a Bucket Count* and *"One Size Fits All" and Other Fables,* both from Thomas Nelson Books. *Only Angels Can Wing It* is her third book; her first children's book, *The Pumpkin Patch Parable,* will be available in Fall 1995. Liz says the best thing about writing is not having to wear pantyhose!

Her professional credits are numerous: she is a member of the National Speakers Association, having earned their prestigious designation, C.S.P.—"Certified Speaking Professional"; she's been interviewed by dozens of newspapers and hundreds of radio stations across the country, including the nationally-syndicated programs, *ParentTalk with Dr. Kevin Leman* and *Talk-America;* she was also a featured guest on *The 700 Club* and *100 Huntley Street* in Canada, as well as many local television broadcasts; and, she is a contributing editor for *Today's Christian Woman* magazine.

Her personal credits, however, are her greatest source of joy: since 1986, she has been happily married to Bill Higgs, now Director of Operations for her speaking and writing office; they have two children, Matthew and Lillian, a cat named Sassy, and a home in the country on Laughing Heart Farm near Louisville, Kentucky.